Limni Korission
Kolpos Lefkimmis
Agios Georgios
Lagoudia
Lefkimmi
SOUTHERN CORFU
Kavos

TWINPACK Corfu

DES HANNIGAN

If you have any comments or suggestions for this guide you can contact the editor at *Twinpacks@theAA.com*

AA Publishing
Find out more about AA Publishing and the wide range of services the AA provides by visiting our website at www.theAA.com/bookshop

How to Use This Book

KEY TO SYMBOLS

- Map reference
- Address
- Telephone number
- Opening/closing times
- Restaurant or café
- Nearest rail station
- Nearest bus route
- Nearest riverboat or ferry stop
- Facilities for visitors with disabilities
- Other practical information
- Further information
- Tourist information
- Admission charges: Expensive (over €9), Moderate (€3–€9), and Inexpensive (€3 or less)
- Major Sight
- Minor Sight
- Walks
- Drives
- Shops
- Entertainment and Activities
- Restaurants

ips on

reas, restaurants, ggested

oking for

ip run rt, weather es.

en each area aps through-out the book and the map on the inside front cover.

Maps The fold-out map accompanying this book is a comprehensive map of Corfu. The grid on this fold-out map is the same as the grid on the locator maps within the book. The grid references to these maps are shown with capital letters, for example A1. The grid refereces to the town plan are shown with lower-case letters, for example a1.

Contents

Introducing Corfu

Corfu is the Greek island we dream about, the ancient paradise of the Gods. With its rich heritage and culture, its forested mountains, golden beaches, unique cuisine and vibrant nightlife, Corfu is a paradise still.

This is an island that has been loved for centuries, by locals and visitors alike. Corfu is 'like a shield on the misty sea' said Homer. It has seduced legions of new arrivals, from the mythical Odysseus to the writers Edward Lear and Lawrence Durrell and it continues to delight thousands of tourists every year. The island copes with all this attention in spite of the ups and downs in the reputations of some of its resorts and despite changing fashions in tourism.

Corfu's breathtaking hinterland of rolling hills and craggy mountains, its olive groves and dense woodlands absorb it all. The fabulous beaches and unlimited leisure opportunities offer choice beyond measure, while the easygoing Corfiots remain ever welcoming. One enduring mark of Corfu's appeal is the large number of foreigners who have settled happily on the island. Today, the market in new houses and the renovation of old buildings by locals, and by visitors turned local, has never been healthier.

Sun, sea and sand are still the basis of Corfu's holiday pleasure. Yet, like few other islands, history has left Corfu with one of the most thrilling cultural heritages of the Mediterranean. The effect of Corinthian, Venetian, Byzantine, French and British influences has given the island a fascinating heritage of buildings, traditions and customs that is overlaid brilliantly by native Corfiot culture and style.

For the visitor, the joys of Corfu endure: the vibrancy of Corfu Town and the serenity of its Venetian old quarter, the brilliance of spring wildflowers in the mountains, the excitement of festivals, feasts of Corfiot food in colourful tavernas and sunset drinks above the shining sea. And always there are those beaches with their clear water under deep blue skies.

Facts + Figures

- **Corfu is the most northerly of the Ionian islands.**
- **The island is 60km (38 miles) north to south.**
- **Mt Pantokrator is 906m (2,972t).**
- **Population: 114,000 of which about 41,000 live in Corfu Town.**

CLASSICAL COUPLE

Corfu has been claimed as being the idyllic Scheria, the island of the Phaeacians, where the shipwrecked Odysseus was discovered by Nausicaa. Several resorts on Corfu's western coastline claim to be where Odysseus came ashore. Let myth and legend draw a veil.

VARIED VISITORS

The Corinthians first colonized Corfu in 734 BC. During the ensuing centuries the island was raided by Spartans, Sicilians, Illyrians, Vandals, Goths, Slavs, Barbary Pirates and Catalans. It was besieged unsuccessfully by the Turks and was occupied by the Romans, Genoese, Venetians, Byzantines, French, Russians, British, Italians and Germans. All of which makes tourism seem very benign indeed.

THE NAME GAME

Corfu's modern name is said to derive from the Byzantine word *koryphoi* meaning 'summit' or 'crest', a reference to the rocky hills of Corfu Town's Old Fortress. The older name for the island, Corcyra, or Kerkyra, is said to come from the nymph Kerkura, who was abducted by Poseidon and brought to the island. There is an enduring claim that in ancient times the island was called Drepane, which means 'sickle', an alleged reference to its shape. If this was before map-making, then the ancients must have arrived by charter flight...

A Short Stay in Corfu

DAY 1: CORFU TOWN

Morning Start the day with a visit to the vibrant market behind **San Rocco Square** (▷ 37), then go through the walkway tunnel behind the market and into the **New Fortress** (▷ 36).

Mid-morning Have coffee at **Bora Bora Café** (▷ 43) at the summit of the New Fortress, then stroll down to Old Port Square. Follow the seafront to the **Palace of St Michael and St George** (▷ 30–31) overlooking the famous **Spianada (Esplanade) and the Liston** (▷ 32). Visit the Palace for an eccentric mix of British Victorian decor and the exoticism of the Museum of Oriental Art.

Lunch Retrace your steps for a short distance behind the Palace and drop down for lunch by the glittering sea at **En Plo** (▷ 43).

Afternoon Return to the Spianada and walk down Kapodistrias Street behind the Liston. At the junction with Voulgareos Street start the **Campiello Walk** (▷ 38), a gentle stroll that takes you to **St Spyridon's Church** (▷ 24), on through the World Heritage Site of the old town and back to the Spianada.

Dinner For the very best in Corfu Italian cuisine enjoy **Pomo D'Oro** (▷ 44) or for a quirky take on some delicious fish *mezes*, try **Peri Dromos** (▷ 44) in bustling **San Rocco Square** (▷ 37).

Evening Wander the busy shopping streets of Voulgareos and G Theotoki for Corfu at its busiest and most colourful and finish off with drinks at **Dali** (▷ 42), the **Mikro Café** (▷ 44) or one of the Liston's many café-bars.

DAY 2: PALEOKASTRITSA AND CORFU TOWN

Morning Take your swimming kit and catch the bus from Avramiou Street in Corfu Town to **Paleokastritsa** (▷ 72–73), Corfu's most famous scenic extravaganza. Visit the Monastery where Byzantine influences and a delightful garden environment are the antithesis of the busy resort below. Break for coffee-with-a-view at the café-bar opposite the monastery.

Mid-morning Walk back down to the beach area and have a swim, if the mood takes you, or go for a **short cruise** (▷ 81–82) to the sea caves in the coastal cliffs. You can also hire self-drive boats if you would like a longer trip.

Lunch The pleasant **Limani** restaurant by the harbour offers courteous service and great traditional dishes (▷ 84).

Afternoon Catch the bus back to town. From the bus station walk along the seafront to the Spianada and visit the **Old Fortress** (▷ 29). Visit the exhibitions in the small museums just inside the entrance and then head for the heights by the lighthouse and a magnificent view of the town and distant **Mount Pandokrator** (▷ 55). Leave the Old Fortress and turn right and go through leafy gardens to visit the **Municipal Art Gallery** (▷ 35) for a wonderful insight into Corfu culture.

Dinner For Corfiot specialties with subtle touches, the famous **Rex** (▷ 44) behind the Liston is the place to be or, for good taverna fare, try the nearby **Chrisomallis** (▷ 43).

Evening Return to the Old Fortress if there is a scheduled sound and light concert, or relax at the **Phoenix** open-air cinema (▷ 42).

Top 25

Achilleio ▷ 88–89 Fascinating architecture, monumental sculptures and a beautiful garden.

Afionas ▷ 68 One of Corfu's loveliest villages straggles up a wooded ridge above the shining sea.

Agios Georgios ▷ 69 This outstanding beach is popular, but still has a sense of space and freedom.

Agios Gordis ▷ 90 A superb beach with great swimming amid an exhilarating landscape.

Agios Spyridonas ▷ 24 Corfu's most famous and revered church.

Agios Stefanos ▷ 48 The sandy bay of Agios Stefanos underlines the beauty of Corfu's northeast coast.

Angelokastro ▷ 70–71 Majestic history and scenery at this ruined castle on the dramatic west coast.

Ano Perithia ▷ 49 A haunting relic of Old Greece.

Benitses ▷ 91 Benítses has recaptured its identity as a traditional village.

Campiello: The Old Town ▷ 25 Corfu Town's old Venetian quarter has World Heritage Site Status.

Gardiki ▷ 92–93 Timeless spirit surrounds the ruins of this Byzantine castle.

Kalami ▷ 54 Beautiful Kalami is linked forever to the novelist Lawrence Durrell.

Kassiopi ▷ 50–51 Once time Roman holiday spot, Kassiopi is still a top resort.

Limni Korission ▷ 94–95 Get away from it all at this dramatic lagoon.

Mon Repos ▷ 26–27 Ancient ruins, a superb museum and woodland walks.

Mouseio Archaiologiko ▷ 28 Meet the Gorgon Medusa and the Lion of Menekrates.

Northeast Coastal Cruises ▷ 52 Get afloat for the offshore view of Corfu.

Palaio Frourio ▷ 29 The fascinating old fortress of Corfu Town.

Paleokastritsa ▷ 72–73 Breathtaking scenery of Corfu's land and sea.

Palati tou Agiou Michail & tou Giorgio ▷ 30–31 Britain's neoclassical legacy matched by fabulous Oriental Art.

Pantokratoras ▷ 55 Corfu's highest mountain-top is easily reached.

Paxos ▷ 96–97 Peace, serenity and scenic beauty in one small island.

Pelekas ▷ 74 A friendly west coast village of great character.

Peroulades ▷ 75 Corfu's far northwest offers stunning sunset views.

The Spianada and The Liston ▷ 32 One of Europe's finest public open spaces.

These pages are a quick guide to the Top 25, which are described in more detail later. Here they are listed alphabetically, and the tinted background shows which area they are in.

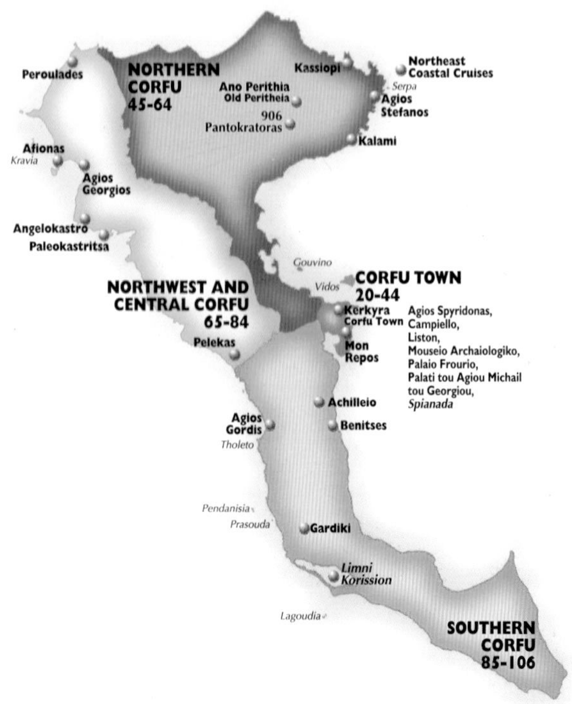

Shopping

Corfu Town is a shoppers' paradise, a colourful cornucopia of retail therapy for all. There's a lively morning market, brimming with fresh fish and vegetables while numerous *zaharoplasteias* (patisseries) and *galaktopoleias* (dairy-based outlets) tempt the most strong-willed. Souvenir choices include religious icons, ceramics, craftwork, antiques, leather goods, jewellery and nonperishables such as honey, wine and liqueurs. Stylish fashion boutiques and jewellers are found in the old marble-paved streets behind the Liston.

Around the rest of the island, every resort has its own spread of similar shops. Corfu is rich in fertile land and in natural resources and recent years have seen an increase in the marketing of food and drink that is locally produced, organic and sustainable. Traditional skills are re-emerging and in hidden corners of Corfu you'll find authentic island arts and crafts of the highest order.

Fashion Feast

Corfu Town has style and so do the locals. The famous promenade of the Liston (▷ 32) becomes something of a catwalk by mid-morning as people of all ages descend on the bustling cafes in the glorious sunshine. All along the paved and pedestrian-only main streets that slice inland from the Liston are dress shops boasting top brand names to tempt

KUMQUATS

Corfu's famous liqueur is distilled from the kumquat, a tiny citrus fruit that is said to have originated in China. It looks like an oval-shaped mini-orange. The rind is sweet but the flesh is sour. The bright orange liqueur seen in a myriad of differently shaped bottles derives its colour from the rind of the fruit and is very sweet. There is a colourless, more potent version. Other kumquat products include marmalade and candied rind.

Craft items make good souvenirs and are sold at shops or markets

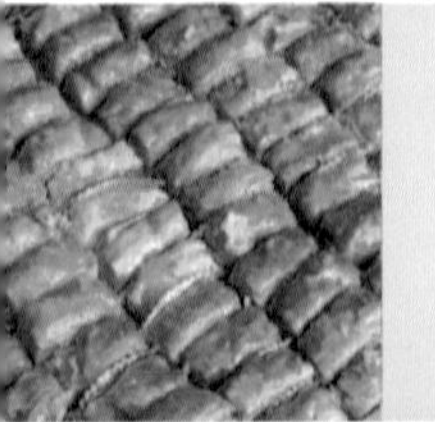

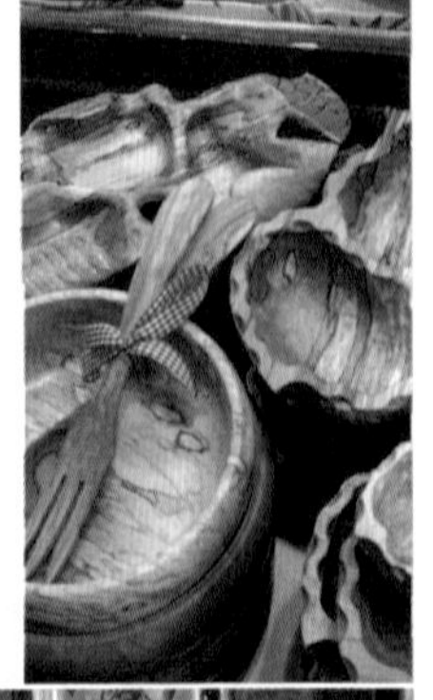

live wood bowls and olive oil are idely available

the fashion conscious. Interspersed with these are numerous jewellery shops with a glittering array of creations.

Liquid Delights

Corfu's most famous beverage is Kumquat (see panel), a sweetish liqueur, and there are specialist shops crammed with bottles of Kumquat in all shapes and sizes. The island produces some excellent wines, including Kakotrigis, a dry white wine with a zesty flavour. Another fine white is Moschato, while good reds include the dryish Petrokoritho. The olives from Corfu's 4 million-plus olive trees were mainly used for lamp oil for centuries, but today, authentic Corfu table oil is available and is a delicious light variety. Many shops stock imported oil so check for local brands, such as the Stamatelos family's Nyssos extra virgin.

Arts & Crafts

Olive wood artefacts are popular souvenirs and include everything from plates, bowls, spoons and forks to candle holders, wine stoppers and jewellery. Top of the range are the pure art objects produced from the knotted outgrowths that often develop on old trees. The beautiful textured surfaces of these pieces can take years of maturing and crafting in the hands of a true artist (▷ 39–41 and 80). Other outstanding Corfiot craftwork includes specialist glasswork (▷ 80) and bespoke jewellery (▷ 39–40) while, at Kassiopi, traditional lace and needlework is still produced (▷ 61)

SOUVENIRS

Souvenirs are often an essential postscript to a great holiday, but you need to be careful when loading up with too many, given the possibility of excess baggage fees at the airport. Many 'Greek' souvenirs are manufactured in other countries and even some olive wood pieces may be imported. You should check as best you can for place of origin and look out for the 'Made in Corfu' label, a mark of locally produced and sustainable goods (▷ 61).

Active Corfu

Bake on the beach by all means, top up in the taverna, savour the sights and shop 'til you drop, but how about a bit of get-up-and-go in Corfu's Great Outdoors?

From top: Corfu offers opportunities to participate in popular activities including horse-riding, golf and a wide variety of watersports

Tracks and Trails

On Corfu, hundreds of kilometres of tracks, trails and pathways will delight walkers of all abilities. The island's famous Corfu Trail runs the whole length of the island for about 220km (137 miles). There is also excellent walking on Paxos. For information on walking check the websites: www.corfutrail.org; www.corfucastaway.com; www.marengowalks.com. For guided walks on Paxos, tel: 6979692713.

Sea Sport

The crystal clear waters around Corfu are a paradise for divers and several reliable diving schools cater for beginners and experts alike. Corfu Divers at Kassiopi have an excellent range of diving options (tel: 26630 81038; www.corfu-divers.com) and there are dive centres at Agios Gordis (▷ 90) and Moraitika (▷ 100).

Deep blue sea and ideal summer sailing weather make Corfu the perfect on-the-water choice. At Avlaki Bay, Greek Sailing Holidays offer dinghy sailing and windsurfing in ideal conditions (tel: 26630 81877; www.corfu-sailing-events.com) and for charter sailing on bigger yachts try Sailing Holidays Ltd at Gouvia Marina (tel: 020 8459 8787; www.sailingholidays.com).

WAYS TO EXPLORE

Try exploring Corfu's network of tracks and trails on horseback or mountain bike. For horse riding try Trailriders who are based at Áno Korakiána (tel: 26630 23090/22503; www.trailriderscorfu.com) and for mountain biking try the long-established Mountain Bike Shop at Dassía (tel: 26610 93344; www.mountainbikecorfu.gr).

Corfu by Night

Night falls gently on Corfu, shops are often at their busiest in the early evening and the streets of Corfu Town are full of people enjoying the evening *volta*, or promenade. Music bars and cafés are packed with stylish young people while tavernas and restaurants do a roaring trade. The scene is replicated in island resorts, and as midnight approaches clubs and dance venues rev up towards the early hours.

Café Society

A famous painting in Corfu Town's Municipal Art Gallery called Night in Corfu depicts the town's 19th century Liston lit by oil lamps and crowded with fashionably dressed promenaders. Nothing changes. Modern Corfiots, like all Greeks, love to linger in cafes and bars chatting with enthusiasm before heading for restaurants and tavernas and then on to clubs and bars. It's much the same in the island's resorts and villages. Join in. You'll be welcomed.

Music Bars and Clubs

Corfu Town's club scene is several kilometres out of the centre along Ethnikis Antistaseos, the busy main road north, also known as the 'Strip', or the 'Straight'. Here you'll find a mix of venues playing modern Greek music and mainstream dance, both types positively rocking by the early hours. Most resorts have a mix of music bars, usually featuring huge television screens for sport features, and lively clubs that can thunder on until the dawn.

rom top: Sidari at night-time; lining at the Rex, Corfu Town; traditional music and dance during a estival in Corfu Town; Kassiopi

ALTERNATIVE NIGHTLIFE

If you prefer a more formal evening out, there are Sound and Light Shows in the Old Fortress during the summer months and Corfu Town's Municipal Theatre (▷ 42) has a programme of classical music, drama, opera and dance. Corfu Town has summer and winter cinemas (▷ 42). For the greatest light show on earth simply take a stroll at sunset at such west coast resorts as Pelekas, Arillas or Afionas.

Eating Out

Corfu's links with Italy and the rest of the world have added sophistication and international flair to a local cuisine that has always been based on the finest natural ingredients and the delicious recipes of generations of Greek family cooks.

Take Your Pick

Greece still has quite clear distinctions between eating places. A *kafenio* is a traditional village café often exclusively male, but in Corfu Town and the resorts, the modern café, or *kafeteria*, is now the norm. A taverna serves very traditional dishes, often grilled meat but also *mezédes*, the wonderful starter dishes of meat, seafood, vegetables and cheeses that can be a meal in themselves. An *ouzeri* or a *mezedhopolio* specializes in *mezes* and such places are often budget-priced. A *psarotaverna* specializes in fish while an *estiatorio* is a restaurant offering international and local cuisine.

Take Your Time

Although tourism has brought a fast food culture and fixed meal times, Corfu eating habits still seem to be dictated by the Mediterranean climate. Breakfast is usually a light affair, sometimes just several cups of strong coffee often with attendant ouzo. Lunch too is fairly light while dinner is late, often not starting until 10 at night and often going on until past midnight. The Greeks are admirably non-hierarchical about dress codes. Be relaxed; dress casually or with haute couture for haute cuisine.

CORFU CUISINE

Corfu cuisine is noted for being among the best in Greece. The island was the only part of Greece to feature in celebrity chef Rick Stein's worldwide television series *Mediterranean Escapes*. Stein made a point of visiting village tavernas that are locally revered for their traditional recipes and locally sourced food. You should do the same, as well as enjoying the increasing number of superb restaurants of international quality.

There are countless tavernas on the island where you can dine under the trees or by the beach

Restaurants by Cuisine

Corfu may lack the international 'fusion' of big city eateries but the island has variety enough to suit all tastes and budgets. For a more detailed description of each restaurant, see Corfu by Area.

BOUTIQUE

Argo (▷ 63)
Bistro le Boileau (▷ 63)
Das Blaue Haus (▷ 83)
En Plo (▷ 43)
Figareto (▷ 83)
Marina Restaurant (▷ 84)
Nereids (▷ 84)
Peri Dromos (▷ 44)
Piedra Del Mar (▷ 64)
Retro Nuevo (▷ 44)
Rex (▷ 44)
Stablus (▷ 44)
Sunset Mediterranean Restaurant (▷ 84)
Trilogia (▷ 64)

CAFÉS

Art Café (▷ 43)
Bora Bora (▷ 43)
Capriccio (▷ 104)
The Drunken Squid (▷ 104)
Eucalyptus (▷ 63)
Mikró Café (▷ 44)

ITALIAN INFLUENCE

La Bocca (▷ 104)
Del Sole (▷ 43)
Elia (▷ 83)
La Famiglia (▷ 43)
Little Italy (▷ 64)
Pizza Garden (▷ 104)
Pomo d'Oro (▷ 44)
San Giacomo (▷ 44)

LIGHT MEALS

Biocafé (▷ 43)
Bora Bora Café (▷ 43)
Cristina's Crêperie (▷ 43)
Evergreen (▷ 43)
Mikro (▷ 44)

RESORT TAVERNAS

Aloha Beach Club (▷ 83)
Araghio (▷ 104)
Brouklis (▷ 83)
Cavo Barbaro (▷ 63)
Karydia (▷ 63)
Limani (▷ 84)
Mythos (▷ 64)
Romanas (▷ 64)
The Rose Garden (▷ 106)
Sea Breeze (▷ 106)
Sebastian (▷ 106)
Thomas's Place (▷ 64)

SEAFOOD

Alonaki Bay Taverna (▷ 104)
Delfini (▷ 83)
Fisherman's Cabin (▷ 83)
Fisherman's Haunt (▷ 104)
Gorgona (▷ 63)
Kafesas (▷ 104)
Kichili (▷ 63)
Spiros Karidis (▷ 106)
Taverna Galini (▷ 64)

TAVERNAS

9 Muses (▷ 63)
Aegli (▷ 43)
Akti Barbati (▷ 63)
Chrisomallis (▷ 43)
Elizabeth's (▷ 83)
Golden Fox (▷ 83)
Jimmy's (▷ 84)
Kalami Beach Taverna (▷ 63)
Lemon Garden (▷ 64)
Nafsika (▷ 83)
Nafsika Restaurant (▷ 84)
Nausicaa (▷ 44)
The Night Owl (▷ 84)
O Paxinos (▷ 104)
Il Pollo (▷ 44)
The River (To Potami; ▷ 104)
Stamatis (▷ 106)
Taverna Bikolis (▷ 84)
Taverna Dionysos (▷ 106)
Taverna Foros (▷ 64)
Taverna O Manthos (▷ 84)
Tripa Taverna (▷ 106)
Vasilis (▷ 106)
Zephyros (▷ 106)

If You Like...

However you'd like to spend your time on Corfu, these ideas should help you tailor your perfect visit. Each suggestion has a fuller write-up elsewhere in the book.

CORFIOT CUISINE

For superb Italian-influenced Corfiot cuisine try Pomo D'Oro (▷ 44).
Enjoy international flair at En Plo by the sea (▷ 43).
Reasonably priced taverna dining is second to none at Sebastian (▷ 106).

Above: Dining out

CAFÉ CORFU

The Old Fortress café Bora Bora (▷ 43) has plenty of altitude.
Cavalieri Roof Garden (▷ 42) for night-time views.
Head for Dali (▷ 42) for trend-setting and cool music.

BOUTIQUE HOTELS

Dreamy décor makes Corfu Town's Siorra Vittoria (▷ 112) the ultimate desirable residence.
For the very best Corfiot style and traditional class, Villa de Loulia (▷ 112) is unique.
Casa Lucia (▷ 110) offers individual cottages in a lovely garden setting. Yoga and T'ai Chi sessions and musical and other cultural events are often held.

Below: The Gorgon Frieze at the Archaeologica Museum in Corfu Town

TIME TRAVEL

Step back 20,000 years at the Gardíki cave shelter (▷ 92–93).
Rub shoulders with a myth-making Gorgon at the Archaeological Museum (▷ 28–29).
Raise your standard at the ancient fortress of Angelokastro (▷ 70–71).

AUTHENTIC MEMORIES

For genuine Corfu olive wood creations visit a local craftsman's workshop (▷ 61) and showroom.

Visit Made in Corfu shops (▷ 61) for locally produced goods.

Make your own Corfu-inspired jewellery by the beach at Agios Georgios (▷ 80).

FAMILY FUN

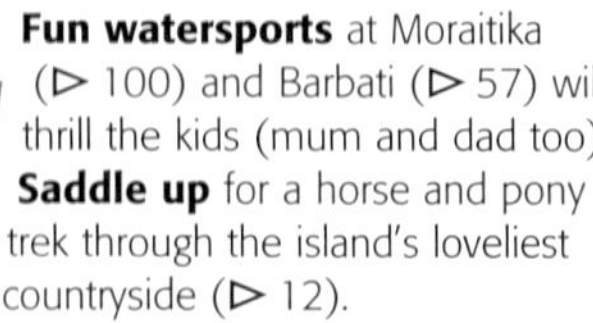

Fun watersports at Moraitika (▷ 100) and Barbati (▷ 57) will thrill the kids (mum and dad too).

Saddle up for a horse and pony trek through the island's loveliest countryside (▷ 12).

Freshwater fun for a change at Aqualand (▷ 81) and Hydropolis (▷ 62).

Watersport fun

GOING OFF THE BEATEN BEACH

Head to Lake Korission beach (▷ 94–95) and walk south until the people run out.

Agios Georgios (▷ 69) on the northwest coast is well known, but still has breathing space.

Avlaki Beach and Kerasia Beach have few buildings to steal the beachfront (▷ 57).

Gaios harbour, Paxos

ISLAND HOPPING

Paxos (▷ 96–97) is Corfu in slow motion. Feel yourself unwind even more.

Unpeel the next layer and head for Antipaxos (▷ 97).

Take a trip to the Diapondia Islands (▷ 76). You'll want to stay.

PUTTING YOUR BEST FOOT FORWARD

High above the crowds at Ano Perithia (▷ 49), tracks wind here and there across the slopes of Mount Pandokrator (▷ 56).
Behind busy Acharavi (▷ 56) plunge into the olive groves following waymarked tracks.
Sample sections of the Corfu Trail (▷ 12).

QUIET CORNERS

Late afternoon at Mon Repos (▷ 26–27) offers peaceful strolls through shaded woodland.
There's nothing gloomy about the serene enclave of the British Cemetery (▷ 34).
Go far north to Cape Drastis (▷ 75).

THE PARTY PLAN

Take it away at the fabulous Au Bar (▷ 42).
Party by the pool – with a couple of thousand new friends—at big venue Cristal (▷ 42).
The beach is between your toes at Edem (▷ 62) where the cocktails are divine.

GETTING A BUDGET BONUS

Careful study of bus timetables can get you, without stress, to the best resorts and back.
Head to Corfu Town's Old Port and beyond for affordable local eateries.
Grab a bike, and advice, on great off-road possibilities.

From top:
A couple walk along a track in Mathraki;
Mon Repos near Kanoni;
night-time in Kavos;
the popular beach at Nisaki (Nissaki)

Corfu by Area

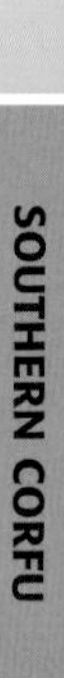

Corfu Town

Corfu Town (Kerkyra) is an enchanting mix of old and new. From its origins on the fortified rocky hills of the Old Fortress, Byzantine, Greek, Venetian, French and British influences have shaped it. Today, Kerkyra is a vibrant and cosmopolitan town of immense character.

5
6
E
Anagnostiki
Etairia Kerkuraiki
Paleo
Limani
Mouseio
Vizantino
Neo
Frourio
Campiello
Mitropoli
Mouseio Hartonomisma
tou Ionikis Trapezis
KERKYRA
CORFU TOWN
Plateia G Theotoki Ioannou
(San Rocco Square)
Plateia
Dimarchiou
Angliko
Nekrotafeio
Mouseio
Archaiologiko
Corfu
International
Airport
Palaiopolis
L
Halkiopoulou
Kanoni

Vidos

Palati tou Agiou Michail tou Georgiou / Dimotiki Pinakothiki

Palaio Frourio

Akr Sidero

Agios Spyridonas

Liston

Spianada

Orm Garitsas

Agios Iasonas kai Sosipatros

Garitsa

Mon Repos

Corfu Town

Agios Spyridonas

The church interior is richly decorated, including paintings

THE BASICS

- b2
- Aghiou Spyridonas Street
- Daily 9–2
- Cafés in Iroon Kypriakou Square
- Good (access is from Aghiou Spyridonas Street)
- Free, but donations welcomed
- There are religious processions to and from the church on 12 December, Easter and 11 August

HIGHLIGHTS

- St. Spyridon
- Icons
- Silverware
- Altar screen
- Church services

TIP

- Move around slowly and quietly, like the locals do.

Regardless of your religious leanings, the Church of St. Spyridon offers an oasis of peace and serenity in the midst of busy, bustling Corfu Town. Locals know this; visitors soon revisit.

Proud landmark The church is the heart of Corfu Town, physically and spiritually. Its slender red-domed belltower stands at the edge of the Campiello (▷ 25) the oldest part of town. The church was purpose-built in 1589 to house the sacred relic of St. Spyridon, patron saint of Corfu, who is so universally revered that he is known simply as 'The Saint'. Spyridon was a Cypriot bishop who was said to have miraculous powers. An itinerant priest brought his remains to Corfu in 1456.

Lavish interior You are never alone in this impressive place, where a steady stream of Corfiots, young and old, pass through. The peaceful, subdued interior of Agios Spyridonas is dense with sacred relics and icons. The air is filled with the scent of incense and candle grease. Silver thuribles and candelabras hang from the painted roof. A stone altar screen of white Cycladian marble is a striking feature, but hidden behind is a tiny chapel holding the silver-encased and gem-encrusted casket that contains the mummified remains of the great saint. It lies beneath a hanging garden of lamps and votive offerings from which dangle tiny silver ships and other motifs. Out of respect, you should dress modestly when visiting the church.

Narrow streets and painted buildings at the heart of the Campiello

Campiello

The Venetian Old Town is where you can become happily lost for a while amidst a maze of tall old buildings, narrow streets, stone stairways, vaulted passageways and tree-filled squares.

Heritage site Corfu's early townscape has long disappeared, but the Venetian buildings of the Campiello survive. These are Renaissance relics whose often worn façades strike a charming note of antiquity. Nothing has yet been sanitized or tidied although the Campiello now boasts World Heritage Site Status and judicious improvements are underway. Shifting sunlight creates a palette of colours across the walls, pale ivory in the shadows and bronze in the evening light. Lines of washing are strung like flags between facing windows. Balconies, stone pediments and medallioned cornices rise towards slivers of deep blue sky.

Hidden corners The passageways, known as *kandounia*, and their linking stone stairways, *skalinades*, are stone-paved and lead to little squares and venerable churches. Palm trees and terraced gardens appear round every other corner and there are cafés, restaurants and corner shops here and there. Local life goes on in classic Mediterranean fashion. People busy themselves amid the cool shadows of morning and by mid-afternoon silence and stillness descends in the baking heat. You can never get entirely lost in this enchanting place. Eventually you will re-emerge on the seafront or in the bustling streets of the main town, certainly content.

THE BASICS

- b1
- Cafés and restaurants
- None

HIGHLIGHTS

- Venetian buildings
- Hidden churches
- Local life
- Cool corners
- Architectural motifs

TIP

- Follow the Campiello Walk (▷ 38).

Mon Repos

TOP 25

HIGHLIGHTS

- Museum of Palaiopolis
- Temporary exhibitions
- Doric temple
- Walks

TIP

- Bring a good supply of drinking water.

The estate of Mon Repos on the Kanoni Peninsula, its villa-museum, ancient ruins and wooded grounds is now one of Corfu's finest attractions. You can spend several hours here, in and out of the sun as you choose.

Royal connections The focus of the Mon Repos estate is Villa Mon Repos, a small, but elegant neoclassical building crowned by a Byzantine rotunda. The villa was built in 1824 for the British High Commissioner of the day, Sir Frederick Adam, on a splendid clifftop site on the Kanoni Peninsula. Prince Philip, Duke of Edinburgh, grandson of King George of Greece, was born at Mon Repos in 1921 but left the island with his parents 18 months later aboard a British naval vessel as Greece banished its then monarch and Philip's

Clockwise from left: The exterior of Mon Repos; the large, airy rooms inside the villa and the shady gardens

uncle, King Constantine. After years of disputed ownership, the Municipality of Corfu took over Mon Repos and have transformed it into a splendid public amenity.

Ancient treasures Mon Repos stands within the site of ancient Corfu (Corcyra) and the wooded grounds contain several important relics. At the south end of the estate are the ruins of a Doric temple of about 500 BC. The villa's bright and airy rooms contain the excellent Museum of Palaiopolis. The first-floor rooms are furnished in early 19th-century Regency style depicting life under the British. More compelling are displays on ancient Corcyra, the commercial life of the Mediterranean world and the history of Corfu Town. Other rooms have artefacts from excavations at nearby Palaiopolis (▷ 36–37).

THE BASICS

F6

Nafsikas, Anemomilos

26610 41369

Museum: Tue–Sun 8.30–3. Grounds: May–Oct daily 8.30–7. Grounds only Nov–Apr daily 8.30–5

Cafés, tavernas in nearby Garitsa

2 Kanoni. Blue Bus, San Rocco Square

Good (grounds); few (museum) Grounds free; museum moderate

The museum also stages temporary exhibitions. Theatre and concert events are held in the modern small theatre complex adjacent to the museum. The only parking available is near the entrance gate and is very limited and on rough ground

Mouseio Archaiologiko

The Gorgon frieze and Lion of Menekrates are among the exhibits at the museum

THE BASICS

b4
1 Armeni Vraila Street
26610 30680
Tue–Sun 8.30–3
Cafés and tavernas in nearby San Rocco Square and on the Liston
Excellent
Moderate
Photography without flash is permitted for some exhibits. Check with attendants

HIGHLIGHTS

- Gorgon pediment
- Lion of Menekrates
- Dionysos pediment
- Ancient pottery and coins

Brace yourself for a face-to-face with the basilisk glare of the fierce Gorgon Medusa at this small but well-curated museum that displays some compelling relics of Corfu's classical heyday.

Great gods Pride of place in the Archaeological Museum goes to the magnificent, and quite scary, Gorgon pediment, one of Greece's finest relics. The pediment was found amid the ruins of the 6th-century BC Temple of Artemis on the Kanoni Peninsula near the Chalikiopoulos Lagoon, where the airport now stands. The pediment measures 17m by 3m (56ft by 10ft) and displays the snake-haired, eye-popping Goddess Medusa protecting her offspring Chrysaor and Pegasus. She is attended by Zeus and slaughtered Titans and flanked by mythical lion-panthers. One glance and she'll turn you to stone. Those glaring eyes follow you about the room and possibly, all the way home.

Lordly lion The Gorgon frieze is matched by the equally splendid Lion of Menekrates, a late 7th-century BC sculpture. You have a sense of a great beast poised to leap as you prowl round this powerful work. Other treasures include tomb monuments, classical pottery, Bronze Age objects and a collection of coins dating from the 6th to 3rd century BC. A third outstanding exhibit is part of another pediment of about 500 BC featuring a pair of revellers, one possibly Dionysos, lolling on a couch amid wine stoups and more mythic animals. They are engrossed in a scene on the absent section of the pediment. We will never know...

The Old Fortress is set on a rocky promontory

TOP 25

Palaio Frourio

The Old Fortress, with its rocky summits and massive walls, is a dominant feature of Corfu Town. You can gaze from its battlements, like some Venetian captain, across the Spianada (Esplanade).

Historic symbol The Fortress reflects Corfu's stirring history, a great bastion against invaders and a symbol of the island's strategic and commercial importance. There may have been earlier fortifications here, but the first on record were 6th century Byzantine, created after the old Corinthian city of Palaiopolis (▷ 36–37) was destroyed by invading Goths. The Venetians replaced and extended the walls during the 15th century and excavated a defensive moat, the Contrafossa. The fortifications that survive today date from later rebuilding during the 16th century. The main features of the fortress are the two rocky hills, the 'Korphyai', which may have given Corfu its modern name.

Breathtaking views Within the arched entrance is a museum of Byzantine objects and a museum shop. Just beyond the archway is the church of the Madonna of the Carmelites in which changing exhibitions are held. The summit of the inner peak, the 'Castel a Terra', Landward Castle, with its little lighthouse, can be reached by a steep climb up ramps and steps past an old Venetian clock tower. At 72m (236ft), the view over Corfu Town and inland to Mount Pandokrator (▷ 55) is breathtaking. On the south side of the fortress is the Church of St. George, a severe piece of neoclassical architecture, dating from 1840.

THE BASICS

- c2
- The Spianada
- 26610 48310
- May–Oct Tue–Sun 8:30–7.30; Nov–Mar Tue–Sun 8.30–3
- Café
- Few
- Expensive
- Concerts and sound and light shows are held in the grounds of the fortress in summer

HIGHLIGHTS

- View from the summit
- Byzantine collection
- Changing exhibitions
- Carmelite church
- Church of St. George

TIP

- On an evening visit, listen for the sound of music wafting from the buildings on the north side of the grounds where young musicians practise.

Palati tou Agiou Michail & tou Georgiou

TOP 25

HIGHLIGHTS

- The Rotunda
- Bronzeware of the Chou and Han dynasties
- The Indian collection
- Porcelain
- Japanese and Korean screens

TIP

- Look for the 'sword coins' and the pierced ivory spheres next to the strange 'doctor's lady' and the colour mixing tray.

Behind the stern neoclassical façade of the Palace of St. Michael and St. George lies a fabulous museum of oriental art that overwhelms the stuffy trappings of British Imperialism that still survive.

Pomp and circumstance The Palace dominates the northern end of the Spianada (▷ 32) and is the most impressive relic of the 50-year British presence on Corfu. It was built between 1819 and 1824 by Sir Thomas Maitland, the first High Commissioner, and was used as the official seat of the British Protectorate and later as the Senate of the Ionian government. The throne room, with its heavy chandeliers, boasts vast paintings of the Archangel Michael and St. George the dragon slayer in monumental mode. The finest space is the rotunda on the first floor, its domed

The Museum of Asiatic Art is housed in the imposing palace. The statue outside the palace is of Sir Frederick Adam, a High Commissioner in the 19th century

ceiling coffered in exquisite blue and gold with decreasing circles of medallions.

Dazzling exhibits Unmissable here is the Corfu Museum of Asian Art, a thrilling celebration of Sino-Japanese art and craft. There are more than 10,000 items including objects from India, Tibet, Nepal, Korea and Thailand. Exquisite porcelain plates, tureens and figurines vie for attention with prehistoric bronzes, coins, clay pots and figurines and items in jade, onyx, ivory and enamel. The bulk of the collection was given to the Greek government in the 1920s by Corfiot-born diplomat Gregorios Manos (1850–1929). Another contributor was businessman Charilaos Chiotakis. A bronze statue of Sir Frederick Adam, the second High Commissioner, by the Corfiot sculptor Pavlos Prosalentis, stands in front of the palace.

THE BASICS

- c2
- The Spianada
- 26610 30443
- May–Oct Tue–Sun 8–7.30; Nov–Apr Tue–Sun 8.30–3
- En Plo (▷ 43)
- Few
- Moderate
- Changing exhibitions are staged

The Spianada & the Liston

The Liston (left); Maitland Rotunda (below); a café on the Liston (right)

THE BASICS

b2–c2

Numerous cafés and restaurants on the Liston

Very good

The Spianada is the focus of all major festivals in Corfu Town. Regular concerts take place at the bandstand in summer. There are useful toilets in the Durrell Garden

HIGHLIGHTS

- Sunwashed Venetian façades
- Local fashion catwalk
- Relaxation
- People watching
- Unexpected parades

TIP

- Be prepared to pay over the usual prices for coffees and drinks. It's worth it for the ambience.

The famous Spianada is one of the finest urban open spaces in the Mediterranean. With its seats, flowerbeds, trees, bandstand, fountain and even a cricket pitch, you can treat it like your front garden.

Flowers and fountain The Spianada extends for more than 600m (654yds) from north to south and for 200m (218yds) from east to west. It is flanked to seaward by the Old Fortress (▷ 29) and to landward by the handsome terrace of Kapodistriou Street and the famous arcade of the Liston. The houses of medieval Corfu once stood here but were mainly cleared by the Venetians to give a clear line of fire from the Old Fortress. The British demolished other buildings to create the park-like space of today. Just to the left of the Old Fortress entrance is a peaceful little garden dedicated to Lawrence and Gerald Durrell.

Cricket and cafés The southern half of the Spianada is surfaced and is punctuated by flowerbeds, trees, a fountain, an elegant bandstand and a neoclassical Rotunda. The northern half of The Spianada is a wide expanse of grass, the traditional cricket pitch of Corfu, where cricket, introduced by the British, was played although Corfu's official cricket pitch is now at Gouvia Marina (▷ 62). With Gallic flair the Imperial French intruded their famous arcaded Liston onto this bucolic space. The Liston is reminiscent of Paris's Rue de Rivoli, a place for strolling along the paved promenade and for relaxing at the arcade cafés and the tree-shaded terraces opposite.

More to See

AGIOS IASONAS KAI SOSIPATROS

Tucked away in the quiet suburb of Anemomylos is the 12th-century Byzantine Church of St. Jason and St. Sosipater. The saints were bishops from Asia Minor and disciples of St. Paul. They are credited with bringing Christianity to Corfu during the first century AD. The church has a fine central dome and patterned brickwork. Inside, there are a number of fine icons and the stained-glass windows create colourful splashes.

c5 Jason and Sosipater Street 8.30–2, 6–9.30 (opening times can vary) Cafés, tavernas in nearby Nafsikas Street 2 Kanoni. Blue Bus, San Rocco Square. Get off at Nafsikas Street Free, but donations welcomed

ANAGNOSTIKI ETAIRIA KERKURAIKI

The arcaded exterior of this handsome building housing the Corfu Reading Society was renovated in 2008. Inside there is a bookish atmosphere and the walls are hung with paintings and prints. The collection of books and manuscripts about Corfu and the Ionian, by Greek and foreign authors, is second to none.

b1 120 Kapodistriou Street 26610 39528 Mon–Sat 9.30–1.45; Mon, Fri also 5.30–7.30, Wed 7.30–7.30 by prior arrangement En Plo (€–€€) Staircase access Free

ANGLIKO NEKROTAFEIO

The English Cemetery was established in the early part of the 19th century during the British Protectorate and contains numerous memorials and the graves of British military personnel and civilians associated with Corfu. In spring the cemetery is a brilliant display of shrubs and flowers. Many orchids flourish and the garden owes much of its beauty to its caretaker for many years, George Psailas.

a3 Kolokotroni, off Mitropoliti Methodiou All day Cafés, restaurants in Mitropoliti Methodiou Accessible to wheelchairs Free

The 12th-century Byzantine church of St. Jason and St. Sosipater

View of the coast looking from the gardens of Dimotiki Pinakothiki

DIMOTIKI PINAKOTHIKI

This excellent small municipal art gallery is approached through a leafy garden. The paintings are mainly by 19th- and 20th-century Corfiot painters and sculptors, but there are also superb icons by such masters as Michael Damaskinos. Notable Corfiot painters include Charalambos Pachis, whose iconic The *Assassination of Capodistrias* holds pride of place, and there are strong portraits, such as *The Piano Tuner*, by Georgios Samartzis. A separate smaller gallery stages changing exhibitions.

c2 Palace of St. Michael and St. George, east wing rear 26610 39553 May–Oct Tue–Sun 9–9; Nov–Apr Tue–Sun 10–6 Café nearby Stepped access Inexpensive

KANONI

The Kanoni peninsula is built up these days, but the southern tip of the peninsula overlooks the two picturesque little islands of Vlacherna and Pontikonisi (Mouse Island). The once-idyllic scene is slightly tarnished since Corfu's airport runway now slices across the adjoining Lake Chalkiopoulou. Vlacherna is reached along a causeway. Boats ferry visitors to Pontikonisi, where there is a little Byzantine church.

F6 5km (3 miles) south of Corfu Town Viewpoint café (€) 2 Kanoni Blue Bus, San Rocco Square. Also small ferries to and from Corfu Town Few Free (small fee for ferry to Pontikonisi)

MITROPOLI

The Orthodox Cathedral of Panagia Spiliotissa (Madonna of the Grotto) is also dedicated to St. Theodora Augusta, whose mummified remains were brought to Corfu at the same time as those of the more celebrated St. Spyridon (▷ 24). The remains lie in a silver casket in the sombre interior of the cathedral.

b1 Plateia Konstantinou Daily 9–2 Cafés, restaurants in Old Port Square None. There is a level entrance through a side door Free, donations welcomed On the first Sunday of Lent the relic of St. Theodora is carried round town

The view from the Kanoni peninsula towards the island of Vlacherna

Looking past a marble bust towards the Orthodox Cathedral (Mitropoli) of Panagia Spiliotissa

MOUSEIO HARTONOMISMA TOU IONIKIS TRAPEZIS

The unique Banknote Museum of the Ionion Bank holds a fascinating collection of banknotes, including a 100 billion-drachma note from 1944, a sixpenny note from the period of British occupation and ancient Chinese notes.

b2 St. Spyridon's Square 26610 41552 Apr–Sep Wed, Fri 9–2, 5.30–8.30, Thu, Sat, Sun 8.30–3; Oct–Mar Wed–Sun 8–3 Stepped access Inexpensive

MOUSEIO VIZANTINO

In the 16th-century Panagia Antivouniotissa (Church of the Blessed Virgin), 90 or so medieval icons are on display in the Byzantine Museum. Most depict saints and biblical scenes. The church is modest in scale yet is quite beautiful. The nave has a coffered and decorated ceiling, painted walls and gilded wood.

b1 Arseniou Street 26610 38313 Tue–Sun 8.30–3 En Plo (▷ 43) Few. Stepped access Inexpensive

NEO FROURIO

Built by the Venetians in 1572 and added to by the British, the New Fortress is a bleak, but fascinating monolith that crouches over the town and commands fabulous views to all quarters. The final climb to the summit is via steep iron steps that are awkward in descent. Head round the back of the main keep to a pleasant grassy area with good views. Tunnels and archways can be explored, but are poorly lit and rough under foot.

a1 Spilia 26610 27370 Jun–Sep 9–9 Bora Bora Café Few. Steep walkways and some steps Inexpensive

PALAIOPOLIS (ANCIENT CITY OF CORCYRA)

Substantial relics of Palaiopolis, the ancient city of Corcyra, lie scattered throughout the Kanoni Peninsula (▷ 35) to the south of Corfu Town. Directly opposite the gates of Mon Repos (▷ 26–27) are the ruins of the early Christian basilica of Palaiopolis. Nearby are the remains of the late 6th-century BC Temple

Interior of the Mouseio Vizantino

Site of the ancient agora opposite the gate of Mon Repos

of Artemis, from which the Gorgon Pediment, now in Corfu Town's Archaeological Museum (▷ 28) was recovered. The sites can be reached along a walkway to the right of the gate of the Orthodox Cemetery at the end of Anapafseos Street.

F6 Anemomilos Cafés, tavernas in nearby Garitsa 2 Kanoni. Blue Bus. San Rocco Square Few Free

PALEO LIMANI (OLD PORT)

The Old Port area retains the atmosphere of an older Greece. The old quays are now a landscaped open square, currently used for car parking. A new marina, due for completion in 2009, is likely to transform the area. Fine old buildings line the inner edge of the square and lanes and alleyways lead temptingly into the Campiello (▷ 25) and to the New Fortress (▷ 36) through Solomou Square with its poignant memorial to Corfiot Jewish victims of World War II.

a1 Spilia Cafés, tavernas in square and surroundings None Free

PLATEIA DIMARCHIOU

The attractive Town Hall Square rises in a series of terraces from the town hall, a handsome building which has gone through several transformations since its origins in the late 17th century as an open arcade. It was subsequently converted to a theatre and a second floor was added when it became the Town Hall in 1903. On the east wall a marble relief depicts Francesco Morosini, Venetian Admiral, later Doge of Venice, Hammer of the Turks in the Peloponnese.

b2 Plateia Dimarchiou Cafés, tavernas around square Few Free

PLATEIA G THEOTOKI IOANNOU (SAN ROCCO SQUARE)

The commercial heart of Corfu Town, San Rocco has little of architectural merit but much of human life. Busy shopping streets radiate from all corners and the Blue Bus terminus is located here. The lively morning fish and vegetable market is reached up Gerasimou Markora Street.

a2 Cafés, fast-food outlets Few

The Town Hall building

A restored cannon mounted on the paved forecourt of the New Fortress

Campiello

This short stroll through the heart of Old Corfu Town, the Campiello, captures the essence of Venetian Corfu.

DISTANCE: 2km (1.2 miles) **ALLOW:** 1.5 hours

START

MID-WAY ALONG THE LISTON
b2 Central buses

❶ Walk west along N Theotoki and in about 50m (55yds), turn right into St. Spyridon's Square. Visit the Church of Agios Spyridonos (▷ 24). Leave by the opposite door and turn left.

❷ At a junction, turn right into the gift shops' alleyway of Filarmonikis. Keep straight ahead and up steps past the Church of St. Nikolaos and its leafy courtyard.

❸ Bear round left and then right beyond the church, and then go left across a small square. Turn right for a few metres and then turn left down through a large square and past the Church of Pantokratoras on your right.

❹ Turn left down steps beside a ramp. Turn right at the second opening and go up steps into Plateia Lili Desilla and to the Venetian Well of Kremasti.

❺ Leave the square on its far right, then turn left and then right into a small square dominated by a huge palm tree.

❻ Turn left at the palm tree and descend a terraced square full of flowers and shrubs.

❼ Turn left at the bottom left-hand corner of the square and go along a narrow alley to emerge in front of Mitropoli, Corfu Town's cathedral (▷ 35).

❽ Turn left up steps and follow a narrow alleyway, to reach a junction with Filarmonikis. Turn right and then turn immediately left past Agios Spyridonas to reach the north end of the Liston.

END

NORTH END OF THE LISTON
b2 Central buses

Shopping

BODY SHOP
This famous name dispenses international aromas just a skip away from the incense-laden air of St. Spyridon's church.
b2 15 Iroon Kypriakou Agonas Square 26610 26979

CAVA KOSTA THYMI
An excellent wine shop where you can get some of the good-quality wines being made throughout Greece, as well as island specialties such as kumquat liqueur.
b2 74 N. Theotoki Street 26610 43159

CAVA PAIPETI
Lots of fine wines including local labels as well as Kumquat, nougat and olive oil soap are nicely displayed in this fine old Venetian cellar. The same management runs another similar shop, To Paradosiakon.
b2 7 Arlioti 26610 30778
To Paradosiakon
b2 12 Agios Spyridonos 26610 38277

CHRISTODOULOS MIRONIS
One of the best olive wood shops in Corfu Town, this little corner of busy Filarmonikis is crammed with olive wood artefacts large and small.
b2 27 Filarmonikis 26610 21937

CORFU HOMEFINDERS
Home comfort zone for ex-pats, this friendly and cheerful place has household goods, furniture and soft furnishings imported from the UK.
a2 1st Parados Mitropoliti Methodiou Street, on corner with San Rocco Square signposted down alleyway 26610 33416

CUORE
There are bright, ethnic colours and styles at this clothes shop which also has a branch on Paxos (▷ 96–97).
b2 5 Agias Theodoras 26610 23370

DIESEL
Hot spot fashion place for casual chic and club wear. Jeans have skintight lines and the tops are fabulously cut and coloured. The staff go with the style.
b2 61 Voulgareos 26610 42023

GREEK GIFTS

Corfu Town's narrow streets of Filarmonikis, Fillelinon and Agiou Spyridonas are crammed with shops that are hanging bazaars of everyday tourist buys. But you can hunt around elsewhere for authentic Greek artefacts. There are religious objects on sale around St Spyridon's Church and colourful pottery and art pieces are available in several wayside shops. It's also worth foraging along by the New Port and around San Rocco Square, where hardware shops sell Greek coffee pots and coloured wine pots.

EX ORIENTE LUX
Towards the south end of the Spianada, among the handsome façades of old Corfiot mansions, is this upmarket arts and crafts shop full of hand-crafted items, including carpets, worry-beads, glassware, silverware, candles and aromatic oils.
b2 8 Kapodistriou 26610 45259

FIVE BROTHERS
This old style fruit and veg shop at the heart of Corfu Town displays its colourful wares, lovingly arranged like a painting.
b2 M. Theotoki

FORUM
Tucked behind Venetian columns, Forum sports the latest must-have bags and leather accessories with a list of advertised labels such as Versus and Laroche.
b2 31 N. Theotoki Street 26610 26979

GAIA
Polished stones, sand pictures, jewellery and carvings, all created from rocks, geological deposits and crystals, fill this fascinating outlet.
b2 39 Voulgareos Street 26610 42622

GEORGIOS N KRITIKOS

A genuine emporium of cloth. Check out every kind of scarf, hat, cap or bag you might ever want. There are clothes also and good old-fashioned bolts of fabric.
a2 42 G. Theotoki Street 26610 37410

ILIAS LALAOUNIS

Subtle and delicate designs in gold and precious and semi-precious stones are the hallmark of this famous-name Greek jeweller with international outlets. Many of the designs are inspired by Greece's ancient cultures.
b2 35 Kapodistriou 26610 36258

KALTSAS

For top-quality, stylish jewellery, watches and other gifts, this long established jeweller is noted for its courteous and friendly service and its exclusive designs.
b2 28 N. Theotoki Street/41 Evgeniou Voulgareos Street 26610 23830/39863

KIOSK

How to fit a huge number of newspapers and periodicals from all over Europe into a tiny space is a well-practiced art in this prime location behind the Liston.
b2 11 Kapodistriou Street 26610 42760

KIOSK POULIS

With local and national press and a good selection of magazines and international newspapers, this busy newsagent just down from San Rocco Square usually has foreign editions the day after publication.
a3 34 Alexandras 26610 37576

KRITICOS

Irresistible selection of goodies to ruin any holiday diet you might forlornly be considering. Charming service breaks down defences more.
b2 Town Hall Square 26610 40444

LACOSTE

The expected confident style of Lacoste offers smart sporty clothes and svelte casuals for all the family.
b2 15–17 N. Theotoki Street 26610 27071

THE MARKET

Corfu's morning market beneath the walls of the New Fortress brims with life and local spirit. A brand new 'designer' market is planned on the site of the existing market. Pagoda-style canopies will replace the old wood and tarpaulin stalls. Hopefully what will not change is the wonderful selection of fruit and fresh vegetables, the odorous but fascinating fish market and the stalls selling clothes and household goods–plus the noisy, cheerful vibrancy of it all.

MAG

Handmade gold and silver jewellery and pieces, often designed on ancient Byzantine templates, are the specialties of this sophisticated venue.
b2 36 N. Theotoki 26610 43580

MARCOS MARGOSSIAN

The exquisite aroma of ground coffee should draw you in to this wonderful coffee-making, wine and spirit shop, which also sells sweets, biscuits and numerous other delicacies.
a2 20 G. Theotoki Street 26610 37443

MARKS & SPENCER

This famous name store is located in a one-time cinema. There's stylish off-the-peg fashion, but not too many bargains.
a2 15–17 G. Theotoki Street 26610 41360

MINISTRY OF CULTURE MUSEUM SHOP

Just inside the entrance archway to the Old Fortress is a bookshop and gallery where seriously expensive art and archaeological replicas are on sale, including large-scale icons.
c2 Old Fortress 26610 48310

MOHAMED KORIEM CERAMICS
Attractive ceramic ware and other artefacts with Corfiot designs are on offer at this workshop.
b2 30 Napoleonis Street 26610 25689

MORNING MARKET
There's everything from fish to fruit and vegetables and clothing here (▷ panel opposite).
a2 G Markora Street Mon–Sat 7–1.30

MUSES RECORD SHOP
Sounds international is the theme at this little music shop. You'll find CDs spinning everything from Irish to Iranian as well as Greek favourites
b2 20 M. Theotoki Street 26610 30708

NOSTOS
Tasty cakes, pastries and a great range of wines and spirits are sold in pleasant surroundings at this established shop.
b2 St. Spyridon's Square
26610 47714

PAPAGIORGIS
A popular *zacharoplasteio* (patisserie) where you'll be trapped by mouth-watering cakes, biscuits, sweets and ice cream.
b2 32 N. Theotoki Street 26610 39474

PATOUNIS SOAP FACTORY
A unique institution, the soap factory uses traditional methods of producing the purest olive oil soap for personal and domestic use. The factory and shop are just off San Rocco Square.
a2 9 I Theotoki Street 26610 39806

PLOUS BOOKSHOP
This Corfu institution specializes in Greek books, but is worth visiting for its delightful atmosphere alone. You may well discover some books in English and other languages, usually about Old Corfu.
b2 2 Parodos/14 N. Theotoki 26610 32200

ROLANDOS
Located in the old stable of the Roman Catholic Church that stands above, this charming little shop is full of colourful and quirky pottery and other artefacts, some from Corfu, others by well-known Greek craftspeople.
b2 99 N. Theotoki Street 26610 45004

CAR PARKING

If you head into Corfu Town by car for shopping or sightseeing, parking can pose a problem. The town is hectic with traffic by mid-morning and the central car parks at the Spianada and the Old Port fill by about 10am. If you are coming in from the north, there is useful parking on a piece of waste ground at the bottom of Lohagou S. Vaikou Street, the street that heads inland and uphill alongside the New Fortress. You can also park in Lohagou S. Vaikou Street itself. Standard rate is €3.

STARENIO BAKERY
Test your taste buds with all sorts of traditional bread, pies, honey cake, and sweet biscuits at this local favourite.
b2 59 Guilford 26610 47370

TOURMOSOGLOU
This small newsagents and bookshop behind Venetian pillars at the heart of town has a good stock of Greek and foreign press, guide books and novels in several languages.
b2 47 N. Theotoki Street 26610 38451

TREASURE
Tucked away in Guilford, this genuine treasure trove of ceramics, woodcarvings, paintings and craftwork has many quirky pieces to tempt you.
b2 Elias Alaifas (near hospital) 26610 33563

TRIFOUNA VOULA
The excellent linen and lacework in this unassuming little shop somehow reflect the enduring spirit and traditions of Old Corfu.
b2 21 Filarmonikis No phone

Entertainment and Activities

AU BAR

www.aubarcorfu.com

One of Corfu's enduring clubs, Au Bar has lots of open brickwork and exposed beams. Music includes house, hip-hop, R & B and Greek and there are some great theme nights. The €10 entrance fee includes one drink.

Off map at a1 34 Ethnikis Antistaseos 26610 80909

BORA BORA

Located at the top of the New Fortress the unique style of this popular venue is enhanced with some fine jazz as well as rock and pop.

a1 New Fortress 26610 41609 Daily 6pm until early hours

CAVALIERI ROOF GARDEN

www.cavalieri-hotel.com

Sip cocktails or coffee above the night-time Spianada.

b3 4 Capodistriou 26610 39041

CRISTAL

Corfu's biggest venue, Cristal is a full-on hot spot catering for over 2,000 clubbers in its huge spaces and round its pool. Mainstream dance and modern Greek sounds predominate. The €10 entrance fee includes one drink.

Off map at a1 52 Ethnikis Antistascos 6932 907936

DALI

A stylish, relaxed café-bar with comfortable seating Dali is a great venue for coffee and drinks to a background of mainstream sounds.

b2 55 N. Theotoki Street 26610 34062 All day

LOUNGE CAFÉ

One of Corfu Town's coolest hangouts with stylish interiors and background sounds that match the fashion-conscious clientele. Great for coffee, cocktails and drinks.

b2 32 Kapodistriou 26610 80670 All day

MUNICIPAL THEATRE

Classical music, opera, dance and drama performances are featured at Corfu Town's theatre. Events also take place at the theatre adjacent to the Mon Repos Museum (▷ 27).

b3 68 G Theotoki 26610 37520

BE SAFE

Night-time Corfu is generally unthreatening and seems to be staying that way. Binge drinking is not conspicuous in Corfu Town and there is not a culture of overt aggressiveness among young Greeks. There is also a mutual respect across the generations. Road safety is a major issue. If you head for the big clubs out on the 'Strip' remember that the road is poorly lit and there's no pavement as such. Get a taxi there and back.

OLD FORTRESS

Open air traditional folk dancing takes place within the Old Fortress during the summer. Performances are given in English, Greek, French and Italian.

c2 The Spianada 26610 48310

ORFEUS

This indoor cinema has all the latest films, usually English language with Greek subtitles. There's a café and shop. Tickets are about €7.50

b3 Corner of Akadimias Street and Aspioti Street 26610 39768

PHOENIX

Corfu Town's outdoor summer cinema is just across the way from the Orfeus. You can sit at tables and order up a pizza. Tickets are about €7.50.

b3 Akadimias Street 26610 37482

VILLA MASADES

Mainstream music is played in this cool, venue with lots of white decor and a fairly fashionable clientele.

Off map at a1 42 Ethnikis Antistaseos 26610 80780 Daily 11pm onwards

Restaurants

PRICES

Prices are approximate, based on a 3-course meal for one person.

€€€	over €25
€€	€15–€20
€	under €15

AEGLI (€€–€€€)

Eat underneath the Liston arches or on the Spianada, beneath the trees. Long-established Aegli offers traditional Corfiot dishes and international cuisine. You may even splash out on *astakos* (lobster) and spaghetti.

b2 · 23 Kapodistriou Street · 26610 31949 · Lunch and dinner

ART CAFÉ (€–€€)

For a coffee break between bouts of culture, or for kicking off the evening with drinks, this pleasant café-bar next to the Municipal Art Gallery (▷ 35) is ideally located in a tree-shaded garden.

b2–c2 · The Spianada, east wing of Palace of St. Michael and St. George · 26610 49366 · May–Sep all day

BIOCAFÉ (€)

Mainly bio-friendly food is the claim at this pleasant little place. Breakfasts and snacks can be enjoyed alongside the stately statue of George Theotokis.

b2 · 15 Iroon Kypriakou Agonas Square · 26610 37761 · Daily 8 to late

BORA BORA CAFÉ (€)

High-altitude pit stop in the New Fortress (▷ 36), this place does drinks and snacks by day and cocktails and music by night.

a1 · New Fortress · 26610 41609 · All day

CHRISOMALLIS (€)

This unfussy, down-to-earth taverna is right at the heart of fashionable Corfu. It serves up reliable Corfiot favourites and tasty grilled dishes.

b2 · 6 N. Theotoki Street · 26610 30342 · Open all day

CHRISTA'S CRÊPERIE (€–€€)

www.christas.gr

Beside the garden of St. Nikolaos Church, this popular eatery has a delicious selection of savoury and sweet crêpes.

b1 · Sophocleous Dousmani · 26610 40227 · May–Oct lunch, dinner; Nov–Apr dinner

BOOKING A TABLE

Booking a table at a restaurant in your home country or city is commonplace to most of us, more so when a restaurant has a good reputation. In Corfu Town booking for the top restaurants is advisable most of the time and booking for the more popular resort restaurants is also advised. But in most beachside and village tavernas they pack you in with enthusiasm and good humour. Just as if you're family…

DEL SOLE (€€–€€€)

This long-established restaurant offers Corfiot-Italian cuisine at its finest. Signature dishes include tagliatelle with shrimps and courgettes, and the Parma ham platter never fails to satisfy.

b2 · 17 Guilford · 26610 32411 · Dinner

EN PLO (€–€€€)

A lovely waterside location for this café/restaurant with views to the Old Fortress goes with such treats as seafood risotto and Cretan salad. They do *mezes*, and sand-wiches and pizzas too.

c1 · Faliraki · 26610 81813 · All day

EVERGREEN (€)

Fast food with a healthy-eating slant, this busy place offers great value salads, sandwiches, ciabattas and crêpes in a lively streetside setting.

b2 · 86 Voulgareos · 26610 28000 · Open 24 hours

LA FAMIGLIA (€–€€)

This is a long-established and popular Italian café-restaurant. Lasagne, including vegetarian, canelloni and *polenta con pancetta* are all available, and there are tasty desserts.

b2 · 30 Maniarizi Arlioti

Street ☎ 26610 30270 ⏲ Open all day

MIKRO CAFÉ (€)
www.mikrocafé.com
Popular with the young, and young at heart, Mikro's terraced garden clambers uphill draped in greenery. Breakfast, snacks, sandwiches, pizzas, crêpes and ice cream by day, drinks and hip music by night.
✚ b2 ✉ 42 N Theotoki Street/Kotardhou ☎ 26610 31009 ⏲ All day

NAUSICAA (€€–€€€)
A touch out of the main town but worth a visit, this favourite offers traditional Corfiot and international dishes with flair. Prawn *bourdetto* is a delicious spicy fish stew.
✚ Off map at c5 ✉ 11 Nausicaa Street, Kanoni ☎ 26610 44354 ⏲ Dinner

PERI DROMOS (€€–€€€)
Adding excitement to the San Rocco eating scene is this charming and stylish *mezedopoleio* offering such marvels as crab 'pebbles', fritters of white crab meat and smoked metsovone cheese.
✚ a2 ✉ Plateia G. Theotoki (San Rocco Square) ☎ 26610 81188 ⏲ Lunch, dinner

IL POLLO (€€)
On the bayside road to Kanoni is this cheerful taverna tucked behind a tree-lined promenade. It serves traditional Corfiot dishes and grills and has great *mezes*.
✚ b4 ✉ 71 Mitr. Athanassiou Street ☎ 26610 26210 ⏲ Lunch, dinner

POMO D'ORO (€–€€)
A flagstoned, tree-shaded terrace and arcaded front underscore the cosmopolitan ambience at this fine restaurant where Mediterranean cuisine with Italian flair is the style. Top dishes include *stracetti*, thinly sliced strips of beef sautéed with mushrooms, celery and pecorino cheese.
✚ b2 ✉ Plateia Skaramagha ☎ 26610 28680 ⏲ Dinner

RETRO NUEVO (€€€)
Opened in 2008 Retro Nuevo offers Mediterranean cuisine with international touches. Tapas and tagliatelle complement subtly prepared meat and fish dishes and exquisite desserts. There's an excellent wine list.
✚ a2 ✉ 1 Solomou ☎ 26610 25028 ⏲ Dinner

MEZES

The name *mezes* means tit-bit or 'snack' yet it sounds much tastier in Greek. (Conversely *feta* means 'slice'.) Mezes can be simple, such as *saganaki*, delicious fried cheese, or *tiropitakia* cheese in filo pastry. Meat *mezes* include *keftedes*, spicy meatballs. Vegetarians can relish *gigantes,* broad beans in tomato sauce, *manitaria*, mushrooms and *spanokeftedes*, spinach balls. Tuck in with the rest of us. And top up the wine and retsina.

REX (€€–€€€)
www.restaurantrex.gr
Rex is an institution that maintains superb standards. Starters include spinach or pumpkin pies. Sauces create such signature Corfiot dishes as chicken in kumquat sauce and swordfish in tomato and cayenne pepper sauce. There's a great selection of Greek wines.
✚ b2 ✉ 66 Kapodistriou Street ☎ 26610 39649 ⏲ Lunch and dinner

SAN GIACOMO (€€–€€€)
This quiet, little eatery, with a cosy interior, on the edge of Town Hall Square, has outside seating in summer and stays open in winter.
✚ b2 ✉ 75 Guilford ☎ 26610 30135 ⏲ Apr–Oct daily lunch and dinner; Nov–Mar Mon–Tue lunch, Wed–Sun lunch, dinner

STABLUS (€€–€€€)
www.stablus.gr
It's top-level cuisine at this stylish garden restaurant and café-bar located just outside the entrance to the New Fortress. Dishes includes duck with cherry sauce.
✚ a2 ✉ 29 Solomou ☎ 26610 35720 ⏲ Lunch and dinner

Northern Corfu

Corfu's northeast coast is where the rugged slopes of Mount Pandokrator sweep down to white shingle beaches and a jade sea. The continuation of the north coast has some of the island's most popular resorts, while inland is the mountainous, hidden heart of traditional Corfu.

1
2
3
4
5
6
B
C
D
P Almir
Orm
Ag Georgiou
Akr
Astrakeri
Akr
Roda
Orm Sidari
P Aharavis
Sidari
Ag
Ioannis
Acharavi
Roda
Karousades
Kavallouri
Sfakera
Ag
Pandeleimonas
Vlahl
Andiperni
Platonas
Lazaratika
Agrafi
Eriva
Episkepsi
Nimfes
Xanthates
Kopsohilades
Ag
Douli
Petalia
Klimatia
Strinilas
Messaria
Kiprianades
Melissoudi
Drosato
Valanio
85
Sgourades
Zigos
Horepiskopi
Spartila
Agros
Sokraki
502
Kastellani
Ag Markos
Troumbeta
Ano
Korakiana
Analipsi
Skripero
Ipsos
Ag
Vasilios
Kato
Korakiana
Dassia
Gazatika
24
Tzavros
Danilia
Gouv
Kira
Hrisikou
0
3 km
0
2 miles

Akr katerini
Agios Spiridonas
Antiniotissa Lagoon
Akr Ag Spiridonas
Orm Aspraou
Pithos
Basilika
N Perithia
Portes
Ag Martinos
Vouni
Loutses
Lafki
Perigori
Anapaftiria
Kellia
Akr Kassiopis
Orm Bolana
Akr Varvaras
Kassiopi
Kato Vodolakos
Avlaki
Northeast Coastal Cruises
Serpa
Trimondi
Ag Georgios
Bralatika
Leondari
Agios Stefanos
Tsitsatika
Ano Perithia Old Peritheia
Sanda
Kokkini
Sinies
P Kerasia
Vor Steno Kerkiras
906
Pantokratoras
Paleo Horio
Vigla
Rou
Plagia
Kouloura
Kendroma
Gimari
Vinglatouri
Katavolos
Kalami
Apolisies
Agni
Nisaki Nissaki
Barmpati Barbati
Pirgi
Orm Ipsou
Akr Kefaloipsos
Orm Krevatsoula
Orm Dafnila
Akrotirio Kommeno
Orm Gouvion
Gouvino
Kondokali
24
Orm Potamou
Evropouli
Potamos
Alepou
Potamos
E
F
G

Northern Corfu

Agios Stefanos

Attractively sited Agios Stefanos is a fishing village and resort

THE BASICS

F2
28km (17 miles) north of Corfu Town
Tavernas
Green Bus from Avramiou Street, Corfu Town–Kassiopi. Get off at Sinies on coast road, and then walk 3km (2 miles) down road to cove
Agios Spyridonas and Kerasia can both be reached from Kassiopi and other resorts by boat
Few

HIGHLIGHTS

- Views
- Swimming
- Exploring
- Boating

Agios Stefanos is a popular resort, but with its easygoing, friendly ambience and beautiful setting it still retains the character of an old fishing village of times past.

Sea and mountains Agios Stefanos is reached down a road that winds for 2 miles (3km) through olive groves then makes a helter-skelter dash down to sea level. The village is busy enough in high summer when boats from nearby Kassiopi and Kalami offload day visitors. Early and late in the day and in the low season, the village slumbers serenely along the inner shores of its quiet bay beneath densely wooded slopes. It faces the raw mountains of Albania, a bare 3km (2 miles) to the east. You could think you were on the shores of a loch in the Scottish Highlands. White-walled buildings with characteristic red-tiled roofs straggle alongside the beach and wooden jetties project into the bay. Fishing boats come and go.

Nearby gems The main section of shingle beach is narrow, but a larger beach lies on the north side of the cove. Boats can be hired for exploring the coast and coves to either side. The road behind the beach continues south for just over a walkable kilometre between olive groves and the impeccable limestone walls of private villas, to Kerasia Beach, undeveloped apart from a couple of tavernas and some villas. You can also walk north for a couple of kilometres to reach the equally isolated Avlaki Beach. Both beaches become busy in high season.

Old buildings in various states of repair are characteristic of Ano Perithia

Ano Perithia

Think medieval and you'll capture the essence of this atmospheric village high in the mountains. Old Perithia was built as a hideaway from pirates—but not from tourists.

There be pirates On most Greek islands towns and villages are often built on high pinnacles or tucked away in the hidden hollows of inland hills. This was forced on islanders in centuries past because of repeated attacks by pirates and by opportunistic invaders. Another reason was as an escape from malarial swamps on the once mosquito-infested coasts. Corfu has several such settlements, which were eventually abandoned during the 20th century but 'Old' Perithia, high on the northern slopes of Mount Pandokrator, is the most famous and is fast becoming a target for redevelopment and tourism.

Old values Today Old Perithia is a compelling place that still reflects Corfu's traditional past. Several of the houses have been renovated, but you can still wander past crumbling buildings that retain outside staircases and the carved brackets of missing balconies. Cobbled paths lead to old wells and meadows that blaze with vividly coloured wild flowers in spring. In the slopes and hollows around the village, terraced olive groves are interspersed with walnut, cherry, almond and oak trees. Towering above is the summit of Mount Pandokrator. There are now four tavernas catering for increasing tourist traffic, but the authentic heart of the village is down in the main square.

THE BASICS

E3

50km by road from Corfu Town on northern slopes of Mount Pandokrator. Old Perithia can be reached by surfaced road from Nisos Perithia Last 500m (550yds) are unsurfaced

Foros (€–€€)

Green bus, Corfu Town–Kassiopi–Loutses service passes through Nisos Perithia, from where it is a steep 6km (4-mile) walk by road to Old Perithia

None

HIGHLIGHTS

- Views
- Old buildings
- Wild flowers in spring
- Peace and quiet
- Walking

TIP

- Do not attempt to drive into the village. Park just before the ruined church.

Kassiopi

TOP 25

HIGHLIGHTS

- The Harbour
- Old Castle
- Restaurants and nightlife
- Shopping
- Boat trips

TIPS

- Take a stroll along the northern side of the harbour to quieter corners.
- Check out the views from the renovated castle.

Kassiopi is the biggest resort on Corfu's northeast coast. You'll rarely walk alone from Easter onwards, but Kassiopi hangs on to some of its traditional character with an old harbour and a historic castle.

Roman recreation Kassiopi tourism has a long pedigree. The Romans built a temple to Jupiter here and Mark Antony, Cato and Cicero are said to have visited. Even Nero passed through on his mad way to the mainland. At Jupiter's altar he performed a song and dance act, an early taste of Kassiopi clubbing. In the 13th century the Angevin rulers of Naples built a castle on the hill above the harbour. The Venetians later half-demolished the castle for fear it might fall into enemy hands. Major rebuilding of the old walls is well under way at time of writing.

Clockwise from left: The harbour; cruise boats in the harbour; the church of Panagia Kassiopitra; the beach; ruins of the Byzantine fort

Faith and fun At the heart of main street is the Church of the Blessed Virgin Kassiopitra, built over previous structures, including the Temple of Jupiter. It contains a sacred icon of the Virgin that is said to have miraculous healing powers based on a medieval story of a young boy who was falsely accused of theft and was blinded as punishment. Some years later, while sheltering in the church, his sight was suddenly restored and he claimed to have seen a vision of the Virgin.

Apart from the historic and the sacred, Kassiopi rocks and rolls as one of Corfu's liveliest and most popular resorts, although its nearby beaches are pebbly and small. Restaurants, tavernas, bars, cafés and shops make up for this and boat trips to bigger beaches are regular during the summer. The town is noted for its fine lace and crochet work sold in long-established shops.

THE BASICS

F2

36km (22 miles) north of Corfu Town

Large choice of snack bars and tavernas

Green Bus from Avramiou Street, Corfu Town–Kassiopi

Ferry to and from Corfu Town. Excursions to other resorts

Few

Limited parking at harbour. One-way traffic system to halfway down main street

Northeast Coastal Cruises

Many cruise companies have outlets at coastal resorts, and on the beaches

THE BASICS

Blue Bay Travel
www.bluebay-travel.gr
F3 Kalami
26630 91158

The Travel Corner
www.kassiopi.com
F2 Kassiopi
26630 81220

Affordable Corfu
www.affordable-corfu.com
26610 97722

Nissaki Boat Rental
www.nissakiboatrental.com
E3 Nissaki
69985 05651

Gianni's Boats
www.giannisboats.gr
F2 San Stefanos
26630 81532

Filippos Boats
www.filippos-boats.com
F2 Kassiopi
26630 81227

Cruises, expensive. Self-drive boats, very expensive

Hop aboard for an exhilarating and romantic boat trip along Corfu's north-east coast. Everything looks so much better from seaward. You can sign on with a jolly crowd or captain your own cruise.

Pleasing panoramas The road north from Corfu Town reveals mountain vistas at every turn where the wooded and craggy slopes of Mount Pandokrator spill down to a shining sea. From seaward the views are even more exhilarating. There is a special pleasure in cruising along the shoreline with the vast panorama of Pandokrator on the one hand and, more distantly, the fretted skyline of mountainous Albania on the other. Along the Corfu shoreline are numerous tiny bays and beaches where tall cypresses crowd down to the sea's edge and where such lovely bays as those at Nisaki and Kouloura become romantic landfalls.

Going afloat From most of the main resorts sturdy traditional caïques run a variety of boat excursions. You can take short trips to nearby resorts or enjoy day-long cruises that include beach visits, barbecues and time ashore at coastal villages. There are also evening cruises to Corfu Town from nearby resorts. The larger cruise boats often have a merry crowd of fellow passengers and the sound of cheerful sing-songs roll across the water. If you want to do your own thing, many outlets hire small boats on an hourly, daily and even weekly basis, although it can be expensive. Registered outlets have reliable and well-maintained boats with a range of engine power.

Zeehond
PETA

Kalami

TOP 25

Enjoying the beach (left); the White House where Lawrence Durrell stayed (right)

THE BASICS

F3

30km (19 miles) north of Corfu Town

Kalami beach taverna (€€)

Green Bus from Avramiou Street, Corfu Town–Kassiopi/Loutses. About 1.5km (1-mile) walk from main road

Small ferry boats from nearby resorts and from Corfu Town

Few

There is limited parking for cars at the entrance to Kalami

HIGHLIGHTS

- Durrell associations
- Swimming
- Boat trips
- Walking

Kalami's most famous building is the iconic White House, once home to the writer Lawrence Durrell and his wife Nancy. Bring notebook and pencil. Write a poem, start a novel—or just dream.

Lyrical words Kalami lies on Corfu's northeast coast in a perfect location along the inner shore of a horseshoe-shaped bay. Behind lie the soaring green slopes of Mount Pandokrator. The immediate hinterland is dense with olive trees, punctuated by clusters of tall, poker-straight cypresses. The idyllic life enjoyed by Lawrence and Nancy Durrell and their local friends and visiting guests during the late 1930s was immortalized in Durrell's lyrical book *Prospero's Cell*. Modern Kalami may have lost the 'charms of seclusion' so loved by the Durrells, but the setting and general backdrop to the village can still delight.

Life afloat The White House, 'set like a dice on a rock' still stands on the south side of the bay. It seems solidly rooted to the rocky shoreline, square shaped and solid beneath its hipped roof. It is easy to imagine the Durrells heading off across the emerald water in their sailboat, the *Van Norden*, bound for Corfu Town. In those days, travel by sea was paramount. It was not until the 1960s that surfaced roads ran to the far north of Corfu. Kalami is a busy place in high summer, but it is fairly quiet by evening. Boats can be rented and the beach is safe for all. You can walk south to Agni in about 20 minutes, north to Kouloura in 30 minutes.

Looking towards Albania (left); the monastery (middle); up the mountain (right)

Pantokratoras

You won't need ropes or ice axes to conquer Mount Pandokrator, but Corfu's highest point makes for a rewarding trip. It rises to 900m (2,953ft) above sea level and will raise you well above the crowds.

Superb views A surfaced road leads all the way to the summit of Mount Pandokrator through a rugged landscape of tumbled boulders peppered with small trees and shrubs. In spring a colourful mosaic of wildflowers adds to the charm. From the summit there are superb views across Corfu's rolling landscapes. North and east, beyond the narrow Corfu Channel, the mountains of mainland Greece and Albania stretch to the horizon. Legend claims that there was an ancient Temple of Zeus on top of the mountain. A church dedicated to Christ Pandokrator, 'The All Embracing One' was built on the summit in about 1347. A small monastery has stood on the summit for many years. Unfortunately, a giant radio mast now overwhelms its attractive little courtyard.

Walking shoes The quickest way of reaching Mount Pandokrator is by car from the south through the villages of Spartylas and Strinylas. Just beyond Strinylas, at a junction, bear right onto a surfaced road that leads to the summit. The final 2km (1.6 miles) is surfaced with concrete, but here the road is tortuous and steep. Parking space at the summit is limited but there is roadside parking before the final ascent, from where it is a fairly strenuous uphill walk. For the dedicated walker the mountain is criss-crossed by tracks and paths.

THE BASICS

E3

Pandokrator summit is 37km (23 miles) north of Corfu Town

Monastery: variable

Café (€) and shop outside monastery gate. Tavernas at Strinylas

Green Bus from Avramiou Street, Corfu Town-Lafki. Get off at junction with summit road and walk for 3.5km (2 miles)

Few

Free. If visiting the monastery, a small donation is appreciated

Annual pilgrimage to the summit on The Feast of the Transfiguration, 6 Aug

HIGHLIGHTS

- Views
- Wild flowers

TIP

- If walking further afield take plenty of water and sun cream with you.

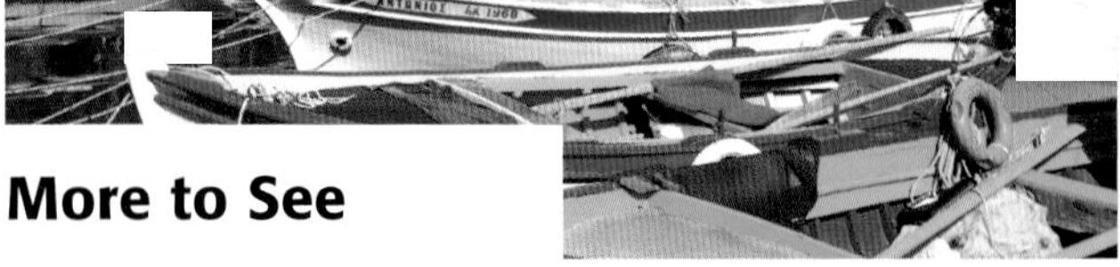

More to See

ACHARAVI

Acharavi has become one of Corfu's biggest, busiest and most popular resorts. The pleasant sand and shingle beach is gently shelving and offers safe bathing for all the family. There are watersports available and beachside bars and tavernas in plenty. The long and busy main street lies well inland from the beach.

D2 34km (21 miles) north of Corfu Town Beachside tavernas and cafés. Restaurants, bars, tavernas on Main Street Green Bus from Avramiou Street, Corfu Town–Acharavi Few

AGIOS SPIRIDONAS

The small beach at Agios Spiridonas has fine golden sand and safe swimming. Behind the beach lies the saltwater Antiniotissa Lagoon a protected wildlife site. Migrant birds include little bittern, plover, buzzard, hoopoe, pipit and flycatcher. Frogs and terrapins frequent the shallows. Orchids flourish here amidst a colourful mix of heather, broom and pine trees.

E1 35km (22 miles) north of Corfu Town Tavernas, Agios Spiridonas Green Bus from Avramiou Street, Corfu Town–Kassiopi. Get off at Agios Spyridonas turn-off on coast road, just after turn to Perithia. Walk 1km (0.6 miles) None

AGNI

Famed for its tavernas (▷ 64), Agni lies at the seaward end of a wooded valley. There is a small shingle beach. The road down is narrow and there is some parking but usually associated with the tavernas.

F3 27km (17 miles) north of Corfu Town Tavernas Green Bus from Avramiou Street, Corfu Town–Kassiopi Few

ANO KORAKIANA

This is an attractive village lying beneath wooded slopes that rise towards the high villages of Sokraki and Zygos. The Church of St. Athanasios has an 18th-century fresco depicting St. Spyridon and St. Athanasios joining forces to banish a 4th-century plague represented as a dragon. Among the more traditional

The harbour at Agni

Avlaki beach

façades the house of the local artist Arestides Zach Metallinos features some diverting nude reliefs. Keep your eyes on the road if driving north: the road zig-zags madly up the curtain-wall of the mountain through 25 hairpin bends to Sokraki—although it's more fun coming down.

✚ D4 ✉ 18km (11 miles) northwest of Corfu Town 🍴 Cafés and tavernas in village 🚌 Green Bus from Avramiou Street

AVLAKI

Avlaki has a wide bay looking towards Albania and there are few buildings to steal the shoreline. Even so, Avlaki can become busy with day visitors arriving by boat from Kassiopi in summer. The wide beach is shingle and is backed by dense olive groves. Avlaki can become breezy and so is a popular windsurfing venue. Sailboards can be hired and tuition arranged.

✚ F2 ✉ 35km (22 miles) north of Corfu Town 🍴 Tavernas 🚌 Green Bus from Avramiou Street, Corfu Town--Kassiopi–Loutses. Then 1.5km (just over 1-mile) walk from main road ♿ Few

BARMPATI (BARBATI)

Where Mount Pandokrator really begins to loom over the coast road, Barbati clings to the slopes, yet it has a fine shingle beach. The bathing is safe and there is water-skiing, windsurfing and parascending, with pedaloes and dinghies for a more laid-back approach.

✚ E4 ✉ 20km (12 miles) north of Corfu Town 🍴 Tavernas 🚌 Green Bus from Avramiou Street, Corfu Town–Kassiopi. Short walk to beach ♿ Few

DASSIA

A long-established resort, Dassia hangs on to its cheerful easygoing atmosphere. The beach is well away from the main road. It is long and fairly narrow and is backed by bars, tavernas and hotels that are quite low-key. There are numerous watersports available and boat trips leave from wooden jetties.

✚ D4 ✉ 13km (8 miles) north of Corfu Town 🍴 Choice of cafés, snack bars on beach 🚌 Blue Bus No. 7 from San Rocco Square, Corfu Town–Dassia ♿ Few

Dassia beach offers watersports and boat trips

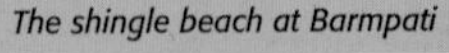

The shingle beach at Barmpati

IPSOS

Known as 'Corfu's Golden Mile', although a touch tarnished these days, Ipsos (Ypsos) is still a cheerful, fun-loving resort with a long, narrow shingle beach running alongside the busy main road. There are water-sports and small boats for hire. All tavernas, cafés, bars, shops and services are on the inland side of the road. There's a lively bar and club scene.

D4 15km (9 miles) north of Corfu Town Tavernas Green bus, Corfu Town–Pirgi–Ipsos Few

KENDROMA

The pleasant little beach and cove at Kendroma lie to the south of Agni (▷ 56) and are reached down a narrow lane. The shingle beach is backed by steep slopes whose dense trees and shrubs extend along rocky promontories that enclose crystal clear water.

F3 28km (17 miles) north of Corfu Town Taverna Green Bus from Avramiou Street, Corfu Town–Kassiopi

KOULOURA

Just to the north of Kalami is this tiny bay with its backdrop of wooded slopes. There is no beach to talk of, but there is a pretty boat-filled harbour sheltering behind the elegant curve of a breakwater. Excursion boats visit Kouloura in summer and the solitary taverna is famed for its seafood.

F3 7km (4 miles) north of Corfu Town Taverna (▷ 63) Green Bus from Avramiou Street, Corfu Town–Kassiopi/ Loutses. Get off at main road and walk for 1km (0.6 miles) Few

NISAKI (NISSAKI)

This old fishing village below the slopes of Mount Pantokrator is reached down a series of steep bends from the main road. Crystal-clear seas lap tiny shingle beaches. Tavernas overlooking the sea and other small, rocky beaches straggle along the shoreline to either side.

E3 24km (15 miles) north of Corfu Town Tavernas Green Bus from Avramiou Street, Corfu Town–Kassiopi Few

The beach in Nisaki

A game of cricket at Gouvia Marina

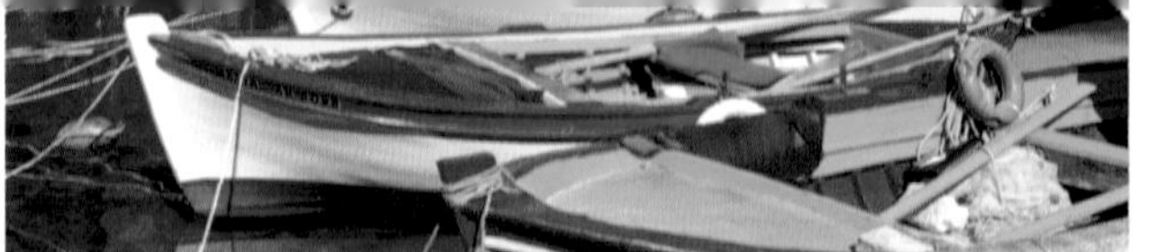

ORM GOUVION

The three resorts of Kontokali, Gouvia and Kommeno lie along the shores of the historic Bay of Gouvia where great fleets anchored over the centuries. Onshore, between Kontokali and Gouvia are the striking remains of a Venetian ship repair complex of the early 18th century. Today at Kontokali there is a big marina crammed with hundreds of yachts and pleasure boats. The resort beaches are small but are still popular and Kontokali and especially Gouvia, have a vibrant restaurant, shopping and nightlife scene.

✚ E5 ✉ 8km (5 miles) north of Corfu Town 🍴 Large choice of snack bars and tavernas 🚌 No 7 Blue Bus, Kontokali–Gouvia–Dassia ⛴ Ferries from Corfu Town

RODA

Roda has become a fairly lively place but is a pleasant, unassuming resort where the original village survives as a complex of narrow alleyways between the main road and the beach. At its heart, beside a little square is the church of Agios Georgios. The resort's long sandy beach is rocky in parts and is made up of a series of small bays. It is ideal for families.

✚ D2 ✉ 37km (23 miles) north of Corfu Town 🍴 Tavernas 🚌 Green Bus from Avramiou Street, Corfu Town–Roda ♿ Few

SIDARI

This very popular resort has several sandy beaches with shallow water, safe bathing and every beachside facility, including all kinds of watersports. Sidari is famous for its rock formations, including the 'Canal d'Amour', once a sea stack pierced by an arch that has long since collapsed. There are excursions by boat and trips to the Diapondia Islands (▷ 76). Old Sidari survives in the shape of the village square with its church, plane trees, seats, fountain and little bandstand wreathed in bougainvillea. Sidari rocks at night with some of the liveliest bars and clubs in northern Corfu.

✚ B2 ✉ 36km (22 miles) north of Corfu Town 🍴 Tavernas 🚌 Green Bus from Avramiou Street, Corfu Town–Roda–Sidari ♿ Few

The sweeping curve of Ipsos Bay

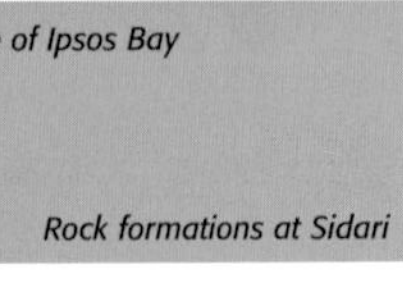

Rock formations at Sidari

Through the Mountains

This route takes in the scenic northeast coast and the twisting mountain roads around Mount Pandokrator.

DISTANCE: 85km (53 miles) **ALLOW:** 6 hours, but more with stops

START

CORFU TOWN
F6

1 Follow the coast road north west for 3km (2 miles) and turn right at a big junction. In about 10km (6 miles) at traffic lights, go right, signposted Dassia. Pass through Dassia (▷ 57), Ipsos (▷ 58), Barbati (▷ 57) and Nissaki (▷ 58).

2 At Gimari be aware that a traffic light system operates, but is not very obvious. Continue above Kalami and on to Kassiopi with the option of a lunch stop.

3 Continue to Acharavi and halfway along the main street keep a sharp lookout for a left turn onto a narrow road, signposted Episkepsi and Agios Panteleimon. Follow signs for Kerkyra and Episkepsi.

4 The road rises steeply through numerous tight bends. Pass through Agios Panteleimon, with sweeping views towards the coast, to reach Episkepsi.

5 Drive carefully through the village and continue to Sgourades, again being very careful when driving through the very narrow village street.

6 Some 10km (6 miles) beyond Sgourades, reach a junction with a road going left, signposted Petaleia and Strinilas. You can divert left here to visit Mount Pandokrator.

7 On the main route continue downhill to Spartilas. From here there are 25 hairpin bends in the descent to the coast. The views are magnificent, but the driver needs to concentrate.

8 A final steep bend delivers you to the coast road, where a right turn will take you through Ipsos and back to Corfu Town.

CORFU TOWN

END

Shopping

AGRICULTURAL CO-OPERATIVE OF NIMFES

You can see the making of Corfu's famous liqueur, Kumquat, at this workshop and can buy the finished product as well as marmalade made from kumquats. It's best to phone ahead for opening times.

D2 Nimfes/Roda 26630 94073

ALEKA'S LACE HOUSE

Long-established Aleka's is noted for Kassiopi's famous lace and embroidery and has a big selection of tablecloths, table mats and embroidered pieces. You can often see local craftswomen at work.

F2 Harbourside, Kassiopi 26630 81402

ART OF OLIVE WOOD

www.olive-wood.gr

For the real thing in beautiful olive wood artifacts, from spoons and candleholders to superb bowls, you won't beat the outstanding work of Costas Avlonitis. There is also a workshop/gallery at Kavadades, near Arillas (▷ 80).

E2 Ano Perithia, halfway between Kassiopi and Acharavi 26630 51596

ASIAN SPA & AYURVEDIC RETREAT

www.ayurvedicretreat.gr

Bringing fashionable facials and body massage to main street Gouvia. The decor, ambience and service are stylish.

D5 Main Street, Gouvia 26610 90255

Mon–Sat 10–8

ATRAPOS

An attractive gift shop with a creative façade, Atrapos has a good selection of colourful ceramics and other pieces from Greek puppets to backgammon sets.

D2 Main Street, Acharavi 26630 64271

JUST LEATHER

As the name says, this main street shop offers mainly fine leather goods, from belts and shoes to handbags, luggage and wallets, with watches as one exception.

D4 Main Street, Dassia 26610 93495

MADE IN CORFU

The Made in Corfu shop at New Perithia on the Kassiopi to Acharavi main road is an experience in itself. At first glance you may think that you've found an eccentric bike-hire company, but the lineup of scooters and mopeds outside the shop are all redundant vintage models. Inside you'll find traditional furnishings. You can enjoy coffee or genuine *tsin tsin birra*, Corfu ginger beer, and sample or buy local food products, such as fig pies. Even some of the furnishings are for sale.

KATERINA BAKA LACE SHOP

Traditional pieces such as tablecloths, throws and kerchiefs are supplemented with some imaginative and colourful creations at this friendly place.

F2 Main Street, Kassiopi 26630 81241

MADE IN CORFU

Right next door to the Art of Olive Wood is this cheerful tribute to all things Corfiot (▷ box). It doubles as a *kafenion*, a traditional coffee shop and as a museum of old furniture and artifacts. There is another Made In Corfu shop at Gastouri.

E2 Ano Perithia 26630 98002

MOONS

This bright, friendly place is a world away from the standard gift shop. Silver jewellery, hand-painted wooden gifts, brightly coloured ceramics, stylish clothes and much more are on offer.

D4 Main Street, Ipsos 26610 93572

NISSAKI FACTORY SHOP

This roadside emporium at the heart of Nisaki is awash with olive wood gifts of every kind. It sells a range of items from simple wooden spoons to more elaborate bowls and ornamental pieces.

E3 Main road, Nisaki/Nissaki 26630 91477

Entertainment and Activities

ANGELO'S BAR

www.angelosbar.com

Twentieth-century retro sounds from the 1960s, 70s and 80s, pop quizzes and mega-screen TV keep Angelo's a popular venue. A range of imaginative cocktails and other drinks oil the wheels and heels.

F2 Village square, Kassiopi 26630 81022

BARBATI SKI CLUB

Launch off with your loved one on a double paraglide, go solo on wakeboard and knee-board, or go bananas on a banana boat.

E4 Barbati beach 69772 26591

BED BAR

www.bedbar.gr

Popular venue for food drink, live music, DJs and parties, Bed Bar keeps on going. Karaoke and Sky Sports add to the mix.

B2 Sidari 26630 99449

CALYPSO

Popular for coffee and snacks by day, Calypso morphs into a lively cocktail and music bar by night.

D4 Ipsos 26610 93571

DAMIANOS

Very persuasive and relaxing all day and into the night venue on the beachfront. A long interior reaches back beneath a vine canopy to the main bar. There's cane seating with deep cushions. Coffee and drinks are the main deal with ice cream as a diversion. Evening cocktails go with easy-on-the-ears music that switches styles with the time and the crowd.

F2 Agios Stefanos 26630 81516

EDEM CLUB

www.edemclub.com

A major clubbing venue, Edem cranks out everything from R&B to Latin, Techno, Trance and House on Dassia beach. Great cocktails, too.

D4 Dassia Beach 26610 93013

HARBOUR BAR

www.harbour-bar.com

Long-time favourite on the harbour at Kassiopi where you can people-watch over morning coffee after a great night dancing the hours away to DJ-inspired latest hits.

F2 Harbourfront, Kassiopi 26630 81227

ANYONE FOR CRICKET

Cricket has long been a Corfu institution from the days when the 19th century British garrison hosted matches with visiting naval crews on Corfu Town's famous Spianada. Today the official Corfu cricket ground is within the Gouvia Marina complex. Here you'll also find the ground of the Croquet Club of Corfu, which has two splendid pitches. For cricket information contact the Corfu Cricket Association: 26610 37520. For information about the Croquet Club: 69949 34352; www.corfucroquet.com

HYDROPOLIS

www.gelinavillage.gr

A well run complex with waterslides, pools, children's slides and pools, tennis, basketball, an outdoor gym, video games, entertainment, children's playground and cafés.

D2 Acharavi 26630 64000 Daily 9–7

PIRATES BAR

www.piratescorfu.com

This hot-spot of Roda nightlife cranks up the sounds late into the night.

D2 Roda 26630 63394

VERSUS

This big main street café-bar has cool décor and comfortable seating to go with its range of drinks. Music is a mix of easy listening to low key dance.

D2 Acharavi 26630 63447 All day

WHISPERS

Diagonally across from Gouvia's church is this well-run temple to stylish nightlife that kicks off after about 7pm. Cocktails and happy hours go with easy listening DJ sounds that range from retro-pop to dance. Dress up daringly.

D5 Main Street, Gouvia No phone

Restaurants

PRICES

Prices are approximate, based on a 3-course meal for one person.

€€€	over €25
€€	€15–€25
€	under €15

9 MUSES (€€)

The Muses offers a huge range of Greek and international dishes in a setting that manages to retain some intimacy despite the streetside location.

D5 Main Street, Gouvia 26610 91924 Lunch, dinner

AKTI BARBATI (€–€€)

Dominating the back beach scene at the southern end of the resort, this traditional taverna serves up a good range of Greek traditional dishes.

E4 Barbati beach 26630 91276 Apr–Oct daily 11–11

ARGO (€€–€€€)

With a view of millions of euros worth of yachts and cruisers, Argo keeps its head with a low key but smart terrace, fringed by palm and plane trees. It's big on fish and seafood, with mussels and seafood platters a specialty.

E5 Gouvia-Kondokali marina 26610 99251 Lunch, dinner

BISTRO LE BOILEAU (€€–€€€)

Cosy little restaurant with classic dishes, including pork fillet with raisins and prunes, chicken fillet with dried figs and walnuts, or succulent steaks.

E5 Kondokali 26610 90069 Daily from 7pm. Closed Sun, Mon Nov–Apr

CAVO BARBARO (€–€€)

One of only a couple of tavernas at this unspoiled beach, Cavo Barbaro has a very friendly atmosphere and dishes up delicious traditional food in a garden setting.

F2 Avlaki Beach 26630 81905 Lunch, dinner

EUCALYPTUS (€€)

Perennially popular harbourside café with a big terrace from where you can watch all human life pass by. British royalty has even been known to pop in for a coffee here. It's good for snacks also.

F2 East side of Kassiopi 26630 81320 May–Oct daily 10am–late

GO GREEK

When it comes to coffee, we are spoiled for choice, and in Corfu, you will always be able to summon a universal 'Nescafé'. But the Greeks know that coffee-drinking makes philosophers, if not gossips, of us all and Greek coffee, *kafes Ellenika*, is the drink of choice. It is served in tiny cups either *sketo* (unsweetened) or *gliko* (sweetened). Never swallow it in one. Sip gently and philosophize.

GORGONA (€–€€)

There's a family tradition of fishing at Gorgona (The Mermaid) that makes for excellent seafood and fish dishes, made even tastier by some subtle sauces.

D5 Gouvia 26610 90261 Dinner

KALAMI BEACH TAVERNA (€–€€)

www.kalamibeach.com

Everything from pizzas, pasta, baguettes and omelettes to the best local fish is served up in a perfectly lovely beachfront location here, just across from where Lawrence Durrell and his wife Nancy lived.

F3 Kalami 26630 91168 All day

KARYDIA (€€)

www.karidia-tavern.gr

Karydia has a strongly traditional flavour with such classics as a *meze* sampler for two.

D4 Dassia 26610 93432 Lunch, dinner

KOCHILI (€–€€)

This long-established taverna has great views. They serve breakfasts and traditional Corfiot lunch and dinner standards.

F2 Agios Stefanos 26630 81700 Daily 8–midnight

LEMON GARDEN (€–€€)
www.lemongarden.gr
Grilled and barbecued meat dishes are the favourite in this garden full of lemon trees; but fish is on the menu, if ordered the day before. Lunch options include sandwiches and salads.
D2 Main Street, Acharavi 26630 64446 Lunch, dinner

LITTLE ITALY (€€–€€€)
This old-established restaurant maintains old-established standards. Treat yourself to such delights as fresh pasta filled with ricotta cheese and black truffles in a Parmesan cream sauce.
F2 Main Street, Kassiopi 26630 81749 Dinner

MYTHOS (€€)
Freshly cooked Greek and international dishes. Try the speciality Meze Mythos (for two), consisting of more than eight starters and three main courses to share, or the Corfiot dish, *sofrito* (beef in garlic wine sauce).
F3 Dassia 26610 97910 May–Oct daily

PIEDRA DEL MAR (€€–€€€)
www.piedradelmar.gr
A stylish beachside eatery, Piedra del Mar offers Mediterranean cuisine with subtle international touches. There's a Greek dish of the day and, on Sundays, a delicious help-yourself buffet.
E4 Barbati 26630 91566 Lunch, dinner

ROMANAS (€–€€)
Known also as Eva's Place, after its formidable owner-chef, this Sidari institution dishes up terrific pizzas and grills with even spicy Mexican dishes on offer as well as delicious home-made Greek desserts.
B2 Sidari 26630 95800 Lunch, dinner

TAVERNA FOROS (€–€€)
Keep heading down between the houses to reach this authentic piece of Old Perithia where the ambience is in keeping with the spirit of the village and the food good.
E2 Ano Perithia 6979 911823 Lunch, dinner

GINGER BEER

The British brought ginger beer, or *tsin tsin birra* as it's known, to Corfu. The genuine article is made from grated ginger, lemon oil, lemon juice, sugar and water. The mix was brewed in cauldrons and although best enjoyed fresh was often stored in stone bottles with glass 'marble' stoppers and lowered into the cold depths of wells. True ginger beer, as still made in Corfu, is not carbonated. Today, authentic ginger beer is made at the Heimarios Factory Kalafationes 26610 33213.

TAVERNA GALINI (€–€€€)
You can select fresh local fish, including bream and mullet from a refrigerated display at this well-run place. There are meat dishes too, and delicious salads such as a Galini special with mozzarella and prosciutto.
F2 Agios Stefanos 26630 81492 Lunch, dinner

THOMAS'S PLACE (€)
www.thomasplace.gr
Once known as Pepe's, this popular waterfront taverna has a good reputation for its Corfiot traditional dishes and its tasty snacks.
F3 Kalami 26630 91180 Greek Easter–Oct daily 10am–11pm; Nov–Greek Easter Sat–Sun 10am–11pm

TRILOGIA (€€–€€€)
www.trilogiacorfu.com
A terrific location at the tip of Cape Kassiopi adds to the fine cuisine at this top restaurant. Starters include aubergine rolls with *manouri* cheese, and baby beets filled with tuna. Or try the *mezedakia*, a pricy but scintillating selection of Greek *mezes*.
F2 Cape Kassiopi 26630-81589 May–Oct daily lunch, dinner; Nov–Apr Fri, Sat dinner, Sun lunch

Northwest and Central Corfu

Corfu's northwest and central areas are where life slows down amid inspiring landscapes. The beaches are some of the best on the island and the smaller resorts and traditional villages are delightful.

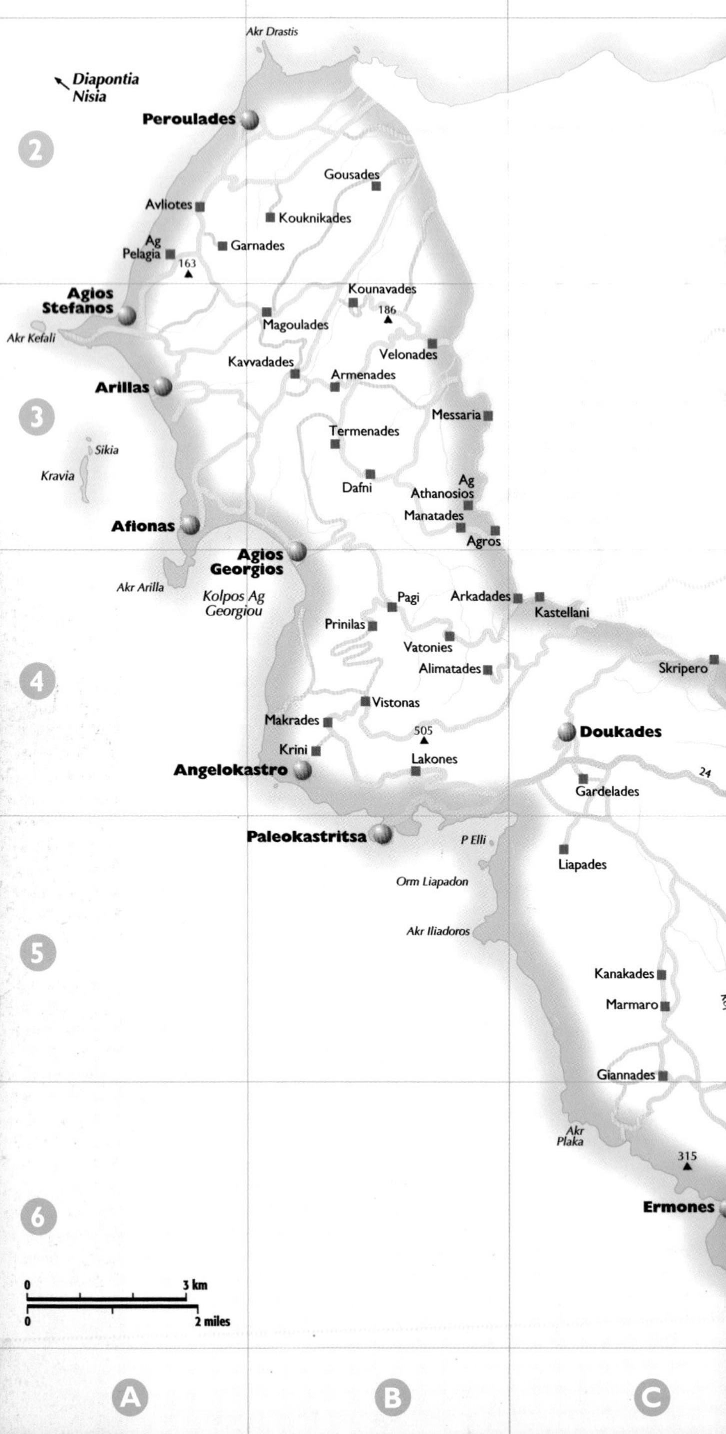
Akr Drastis
Diapontia Nisia
Peroulades
2
Gousades
Avliotes
Kouknikades
Ag Pelagia
Garnades
163
Agios Stefanos
Kounavades
186
Magoulades
Akr Kefali
Velonades
Kavvadades
Armenades
Arillas
3
Messaria
Termenades
Sikia
Kravia
Dafni
Ag Athanosios
Manatades
Afionas
Agros
Agios Georgios
Akr Arilla
Kolpos Ag Georgiou
Pagi
Arkadades
Kastellani
Prinilas
Vatonies
Alimatades
Skripero
4
Vistonas
Makrades
505
Doukades
Krini
Lakones
Angelokastro
24
Gardelades
Paleokastritsa
P Elli
Liapades
Orm Liapadon
Akr Iliadoros
5
Kanakades
Marmaro
Giannades
Akr Plaka
315
6
Ermones
0
3 km
0
2 miles
A
B
C

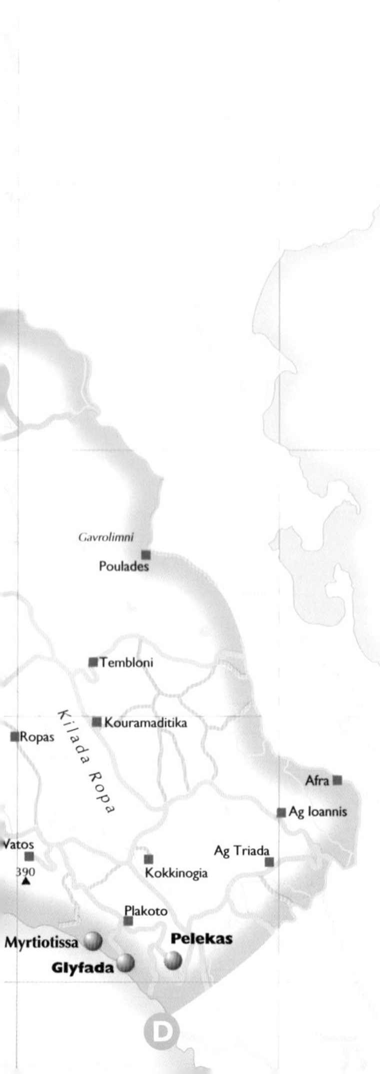
Gavrolimni
Poulades
Tembloni
Kilada Ropa
Kouramaditika
Ropas
Afra
Ag Ioannis
Ag Triada
390
Kokkinogia
Plakoto
Myrtiotissa
Pelekas
Glyfada
D
E

Afionas

The church in the village (left); a white-washed house (right)

THE BASICS

A3
26km (16 miles) northwest of Corfu Town
Cafés and tavernas
Green bus from Avramiou Street, Corfu Town–Magoulades–Afionas
Few

HIGHLIGHTS

- Views
- Relaxing
- Wild walks
- Swimming

TIP

- It's a pleasant and easy walk to nearby Agios Georgios (▷ 69).

Afionas is not a beach resort, but for determined Greek Gods there are two fine little beaches just down a rough and rocky path on the beautiful Cape Arillas.

Ancient settlers Where Afionas ends Cape Arillas begins. The area is rich in ancient myths and tangled history. Excavations in 1912 uncovered the remains of a 3000BC neolithic settlement on the headland and ruined walls, dating from around 500BC, attest to the area's antiquity. The views from Afionas are breathtaking.

Due west is Gravia Island, or 'Ship Island' with its little galaxy of islets trailing like caïques behind it. To the north, more distantly, are the Diapondia Islands (▷ 76), Erikoussa, Othoni and Mathraki. The view to the south and east is even more dramatic, a panorama across a great bay to the long beach of Agios Georgios and then sweeping up towards Mount Pantokrator and south to Cape Falakron.

Out and about From the road end in Afionas, where a cluster of attractive buildings includes the small church of Agios Giannos, a path leads onto Cape Arillas proper. The path leads down the spine of the promontory. Near its end is a narrow neck of scrubby land that links the rocky hills of the ridge.

Small beaches lie to either side and you can switch from one to the other depending on the wind direction on this often breezy coast. Afionas has several outstanding tavernas and restaurants.

Agios Georgios beach (left); a view of Agios Georgios from Afionas (right)

Agios Georgios

This northwest resort has an enticing air about it. It takes a bit of determination to get here and once you arrive, there seems no point in leaving too soon.

Best Beach At Agios Georgios a crescent of golden sand sweeps invitingly for 3km (2 miles) between Cape Arillas (▷ 76) to the north and Cape Falakron to the south. The beach is pebbly in places just offshore and like all the beaches along this rugged coast things can become a touch breezy at times. But it's a warm breeze and nothing can mar the vast panorama of sea and sky and the sense of freedom it all brings. The beach is generally ideal for families, but it does shelf unexpectedly in places, so watch young children. Local custom over the years spared Agios Georgios from a continuous beachside road. Access roads lead from inland directly to the sea, and this heightens the resort's distinctiveness.

Watersports and walking Agios Georgios is a windsurfing centre, ideal for beginners and experts, and there are wind surfing schools and rental outfits on the beach as well as jet-ski and water-ski hire. Cape Arillas (▷ 76) thrusts south from the northern edge of the bay and can be easily reached on foot as can neighbouring Afionas (▷ 68) itself.

Agios Georgios is not geared to full blast socializing but there are plenty of tavernas, cafés, and snack bars alongside the beach. The fascinating jewellery workshop of Ilios (▷ 80) at the southern end of the beach is a rewarding visit.

THE BASICS

B4

25km (15.5 miles) northwest of Corfu Town

Choice of several tavernas and restaurants throughout the resort

Corfu Town–Agios Georgios–Pagi. Green Bus (two per day)

Few

HIGHLIGHTS

- Swimming
- Views
- Watersports
- Exploring

Angelokastro

TOP 25

HIGHLIGHTS

- Views
- Sense of history
- Spectacular landscapes
- Wildflowers
- Peace and quiet

TIPS

- Great care should be taken when close to the unprotected cliff edges, especially if accompanied by children.
- Keep your head down when going through the church doorway.

The ruined 12th-century castle of Angelokastro is where you really feel the awesome history of Corfu in your bones. It's a stiff hike up hundreds of steps, so sympathize with ancient invaders.

Island defence Angelokastro seems to have been named after the Comneni family, who ruled Corfu at the time. The castle played a key role in the successful defence of the island for hundreds of years. From Angelokastro, a guard was kept over the west coast where invaders might easily come ashore. A fierce siege by the Venetians in 1386 against a last stand by Corfu's Angevin rulers lasted nearly a year. Unsuccessful sieges by Turkish invaders took place in 1537, 1571 and 1716. Military use of Angelokastro ended in the 19th century during the British Protectorate.

Clockwise from left: The ruins of Angelokastro; views from the ruins; looking up at the castle; the church of Agia Kyriaki on the site

High cliffs Today the ruined walls of the castle survive on the rocky heights whose seaward cliffs drop 300m (984ft) into the sea. Rough steps wind steeply from a car park to a postern gate into the inner keep. Relics lie scattered across the hilltop. The tiny church of the Archangels Michael and Gabriel dates from 1784 when it was rebuilt on an older structure. In front of the church are seven grave moulds cut into the rock. The views to seaward are spectacular. East of the summit, and at a lower level, are underground water cisterns and in the lower keep is a cave that became a chapel to St. Kyriaki in the late 18th century.

Today The castle structure is dangerous—renovation work has been planned but not begun. Entry to the site is possible, but the authorities take no responsbility for the safety of visitors.

THE BASICS

- B4
- 28km (17 miles) northwest of Corfu Town
- Apr–Oct daily 8.30–3, but check locally before visiting—the site is intermittently closed for repairs
- Angelokastro Taverna (€–€€)
- Green Bus from Avramiou Street, Corfu Town–Makrades, then 2.5km (1.5-mile) walk
- None
- Inexpensive

Paleokastritsa

HIGHLIGHTS

- The monastery
- Beaches
- Boat trips
- Mountain views

TIP

- For photographs of a richer hue, visit the monastery in the late afternoon.

Prepare to have your breath taken away by the sheer beauty of Paleokastritsa, favourite picnic spot of the British hierarchy during the protectorate and now playground for the rest of us.

Ancient myths Soaring mountains, swathed in trees and studded with rocky cliffs, loom over the lagoon-like bays and silvery beaches of Paleokastritsa.

Yet long before today's sightseers, Paleokastritsa was revered as a religious centre, the home of the Monastery of the Virgin Mary, or the 'Virgin of the Old Castle' from which the name Paleokastritsa comes. It has been suggested that Paleokastritsa was the site of the ancient castle and city of Alcinoös, King of the Phaeacians, the legendary inhabitants of Scheria, ancient Corfu.

Clockwise from left: The sandy beaches and coves at Paleokastritsa; Paleokastritsa monastery; the altarpiece inside the monastery; the beautiful beach

Visiting today The present monastery dates mainly from the 18th century. The walls of its tiny church are thick with icons in heavy frames. A fine painting of the *Last Judgement* lies above the south doorway. The church is approached through a garden terrace from where there are breathtaking views across the Bay of Liapades to Cape Agios Iliodoros. There are flowers, lemon trees and bougainvillea throughout the complex. Inside the monastery is an oil mill and a little museum displaying icons, shells and bones from the sea.

Today Paleokastritsa is famed more for its small, but beautiful beaches and for the beauty of its wooded headlands and crystal seas. Beach and watersport equipment can be rented and boats can be hired. There are organized boat trips along the coast and to sea caves. The clear seas round Paleokastritsa are popular with scuba divers.

THE BASICS

- B5
- 25km (15.5 miles) northwest of Corfu Town
- Numerous tavernas and cafés
- Green bus from Avramiou Street, Corfu Town–Paleokastritsa
- Few

Pelekas

The sun sets near Pelekas (left); Kaiser's Throne viewpoint near Pelekas (below)

THE BASICS

- D6
- 18km (11 miles) west of Corfu Town
- Numerous tavernas and cafés in the village and at beaches
- Blue Bus No. 11 from San Rocco Square
- Few

HIGHLIGHTS

- Panoramic views
- Village ambience
- Great beaches
- Walking

TIP

- There are private car parks behind the beaches. Prices average €4.

There is a delightful laid-back atmosphere at hilltop Pelekas. The village is tucked away on Corfu's west coast above a number of beaches that were once the secret getaways of determined sunseekers.

Traditional village Pelekas straggles down the side of a tree-covered hill and above steep slopes that plunge down to the sea and to a succession of fine beaches. The village is a charming place and has a central square where the fat casing of an old sea mine, painted in the Greek colours of blue and white, serves as an eccentric plant pot. A narrow road winds uphill from the centre of Pelekas, past a little church with detached bell tower, to the hilltop Levant Hotel and Sunset Mediterranean Restaurant (▷ 84).

Great views Behind the hotel a paved path leads to a railed viewpoint like the conning tower of a submarine, but with seats. From here there are fabulous views all the way to Corfu Town in the east, along the Ropa Valley to the north and of the mountain of Agios Mattheos to the south. Famous above all are the sunset views across the sea to the west. This was the favourite spot of Kaiser Wilhelm II who used to motor across the island from the Achilleon Palace (▷ 88–89). The beaches of Gialiskari and Kontogialos are reached down steep and winding roads. Both beaches have all the usual hire equipment and beachside tavernas and bars. A small local bus runs from the village to the beaches in summer.

Village homes (left and middle); the belltower in the heart of the village (right)

Peroulades

The old village of Peroulades lies in the far north west corner of Corfu. High sandstone cliffs rise abruptly from the sea above narrow pebble beaches and you begin to wonder where all the other people have got to.

Remote cliffs Peroulades is slowly recovering from a long period of decline and a traditional economy of smallholding survives amid the surrounding countryside. The village has a slightly worn look although its architectural heritage of Venetian buildings and façades is increasingly recognized. North of Peroulades is Akra (Cape) Drastis, a lonely headland of cream-coloured sandstone cliffs and sea stacks crowned with thick, spiky undergrowth. A surfaced road leads from the centre of the village out towards the cape and eventually becomes an unsurfaced but firm track that leads down to tiny coves.

Sunset views West of Peroulades is the famous Longas or 'Sunset Beach' and cliffs. From the cliff top, concrete steps wind down to the base of 50m (170ft) high cliffs and a narrow strip of pebble and sand beach that can be doused by onshore waves in fierce winds.

You can find peace and quiet around Cape Drastis and at Longas in the off season, but a popular taverna dominates the Longas clifftop. It offers superb views along with food and drink and musical accompaniment to the sunset experience. There is parking at the cliff top, but the edge is unprotected.

THE BASICS

B2

45km (28 miles) northwest of Corfu Town

Panorama Restaurant/ Seventh Heaven Café

Green Bus from Avramiou Street, Corfu Town–Sidari–Peroulades–Agios Stefanos

Access by road and track to clifftop Longas

HIGHLIGHTS

- Traditional village
- Lonely Cape Drastis
- Sunset views
- Welcome breezes

TIP

- Be very careful if parking at the unprotected cliff edge.

More to See

AGIOS STEFANOS

Agios Stefanos has one of the widest, flattest beaches in Corfu. Beyond its little church is a large harbour full of fishing caïques and excursion boats. Ferries to the Diapontia Islands leave from here. Apart from the superb beach, the area is good for pleasant, but fairly robust walking, both along the coast to either side or inland.

A3 45km (28 miles) northwest of Corfu Town Cafés and tavernas Green bus from Avramiou Street, Corfu Town–Sidari–Agios Stefanos Ferry to Diapondia Islands and to Paleokastritsa Few

ARILLAS

Arillas lies at the northern end of a broad bay and is a pleasant, fairly low key resort, but with several excellent cafés, bars and tavernas. The narrow sand and shingle beach slopes gently. The bay can be breezy at times but it all adds to the fresh and friendly feel of the resort and makes Arillas an ideal spot for windsurfers. Boards, pedaloes, and canoes can be hired.

A3 30km (19 miles) northwest of Corfu Town Cafés and tavernas Green bus from Avramiou Street, Corfu Town–Afionas continues to Arillas Good

DIAPONTIA NISIA (DIAPONDIA ISLANDS)

The islands lie about 10km (6 miles) from Cape Drastis (▷ 75). The main islands are Erikoussa, Othoni and Mathraki. All the islands have beaches and some tavernas and rooms to let.

Off map at A2 10km (6 miles) north-west of Corfu Island Cafés and tavernas Ferries from Agios Stefanos, Sidari mainly during summer months. Regular passenger ferries and twice-weekly car ferries from Corfu Town Few ? Sea crossing can be rough

DOUKADES

From the north, Doukades seems to huddle beneath a vast overhanging mountain. Close up you find a charming traditional village and the mountain has become a peaceful backdrop of steep slopes, dense with olive groves, cypresses and holm oaks. Throughout the village are Venetian

Aqualand, near Ermones

A quiet street in Doukades

buildings that have retained their elegant façades.

C4 18km (11 miles) northwest of Corfu Town Tavernas Green bus from Avramiou Street, Corfu Town–Paleokastritsa, then an 0.5km (0.25-mile) uphill walk Few Feast of St. John, late Jun

ERMONES

Ermones is hedged round with development, huge hotels having laid claim to the terraced slopes that loom over the bay. The shingle beach, lapped by a turquoise sea, is quite small and is crowded in high season, but there are numerous activities at hand, including paragliding and scuba diving.

C6 17km (10.5 miles) west of Corfu Town Tavernas Green bus from Avramiou Street, Corfu Town (3 direct buses a day Few The beach shelves quickly into deep water; take care with children

GLYFADA

This popular resort is reached down a wildly winding road. The long sandy beach is backed by tree-covered coastal hills, but beachside development has increased. Pleasant walks can be made to north and south.

D6 16km (10 miles) west of Corfu Town Tavernas and café-bars Green bus from Avramiou Street, Corfu Town-Vatos-Glyfada Few The beach shelves steeply in places but there are safe areas for youngsters

MYRTIOTISSA

The sea is slowly eating away at Myrtiotissa's already narrow beach, but this is still an atmospheric venue. Today, there's a cheerful mix of the clothed and unclothed of all ages. There can be strong currents offshore. At the beach's northern end the Monastery of the Blessed Virgin Myrtiotissa has arched doorways and carved keystones of some style.

D6 12km (7.5 miles) west of Corfu Town Taverna Green bus from Avramiou Street, Corfu Town–Vato, from where it is a 2.5km (1.5-mile) walk None Steep, concrete road to the beach. Best to park at the official car park above the beach from where it is about a 1km (0.6-mile) hike.

The island of Mathraki

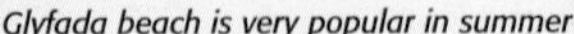

Glyfada beach is very popular in summer

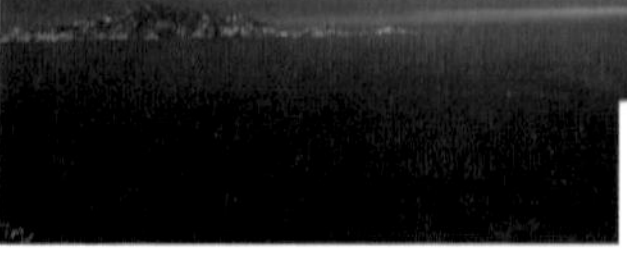

Headland and Hidden Chapel

This is a fascinating walk on one of Corfu's most striking natural features, Cape Arillas. Parts of the path are very rocky.

DISTANCE: 3.25km (2 miles) **ALLOW:** 2 hours with a swimming stop

START

AFIONAS VILLAGE SQUARE
A3 Green bus

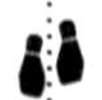

❶ At the very top of the village and just past the church, turn left, signposted 'To St. Stilianos Cave and Porto Timoni Beach'. Follow a roughly surfaced path.

❷ Keep straight ahead where the path becomes rocky. The path descends steadily from here.

❸ Abreast of the exposed end of a broken wall, the path zig-zags and then divides. Take the left-hand branch and descend quite steeply but safely over broken rocks.

❹ The path levels off for a while and then descends to the sandy neck of the peninsula and to a pair of little beaches at Porto Timoni. You can stop for a swim or wait until your return. From the beaches follow a less rocky path farther out towards the headland.

❺ The path winds through shrubs and flowers that exude a delightful aroma. Cross a narrow section with care and then follow an easier path above a lagoon-like bay.

❻ Follow the rising path towards the far headland and where it divides, take the left-hand branch uphill to reach the cave of St. Stilianos, where a little door in the rock face opens into a tiny chapel.

❼ Retrace your steps to the junction. The other branch is a dead end. Go right and continue to Porto Timoni and the tempting little beaches.

❽ Follow the steep rocky path back uphill to Afionas.

AFIONAS VILLAGE SQUARE

END

Shopping

THE ART OF OLIVE WOOD

www.olive-wood.gr
This is the workshop of artist-craftsman Costas Avlonitis, who also has a gallery-shop at New Perithia on the north coast. The workshop is in a lovely location framed by olive trees and the gallery is full of superb olive wood artefacts.
B3 Kavvadades
26630 51596

BITRO: PERDITA'S GLASS ART

www.perditasglassart.com
Just by the junction of the road to the beach is this showroom for Perdita Mouzakiti's unique glass-work. Signature pieces include coloured glass worked into old Byzantine tiles to make wall hangings and lights. There are smaller pieces and jewellery.
A3 Agios Stefanos
26630 51384

GOLDEN FOX

www.corfugoldenfox.com
Also a restaurant, the Golden Fox has a shop with rugs, fine lace, linen and hand-carved olive wood objects.
B4 Lakones 26630 49101

ILIOS

www.ilios-living-art.com
Outstanding jewellery pieces are made in an inspiring workshop and gallery environment.
B4 Agios Georgios, south end 26630 96043

KIR ART

Adding to the creative magic of the area is this fascinating gallery and workshop where striking pieces in stainless steel and olive wood are produced, as well as paintings and collages.
B4 Agios Georgios, north end 26630 51925

MAKRADES

The little village of Makrades lies on the road north from Paleokastritsa to the Troumbeta Pass and is the gateway to Angelokastro (▷ 70–71). It also bids to be the retail hub of the world, with a swath of roadside stalls selling knitwear, embroidered table linen, ceramics and carpets, and natural products like honey and wine. Bargain with the stallholders.
B4

ARTS & CRAFTS

There must be something in the air in the far northwest corner of Corfu, where there seems to be a quiet revolution in the production of high-quality creative arts and crafts. The Art of Olive Wood produces authentic Corfiot products with great originality; Perdita's Glass Art is unique and the work of Kir Art is equally so. Ilios Living Art shines among it all. Here in their gallery-workshop above the beach, young goldsmiths and jewellers creat marvellous pieces. They also stage seminars where visitors take the first step in creating bespoke jewellery and can take home their own creations. Ilios also hosts events, exhibitions, readings and concerts.

MONASTERY SHOP

At the heart of the beautiful Monastery of the Virgin Mary at Paleokastritsa is a little outlet that sells various handmade items and the monks' own olive oil.
B5 Monastery of the Virgin Mary, Paleokastritsa

OLIVEN UND MEHR

www.olivenundmeer.de
This attractive shop in the village square at Afionas sells olive-themed products from oil and tapenade to pottery, linen, kitchen utensils and soap.
A3 Afionas 26630 52081

TRIKLINO VINEYARD

www.triklinovineyard.gr
Get an idea of traditional agricultural techniques and take a stroll around the vineyards at this winery that produces vintage from local grape varieties. A video shows the production process of wine and olive oil. Local food products are also on sale.
B5 Karoubatika, Paleokastritsa 26610 58184 Tue–Sat noon–7

Entertainment and Activities

ACHILLION DIVING CENTRE
www.diving-corfu.com
Based at Ermones and Paleokastritsa, this centre runs diving trips and courses.
B5 Akrotiri Beach Hotel, Paleokastritsa 693 272 9011 (mobile)

ALOHA BEACH CLUB
An all-day venue offering snacks and *mezes* in the evenings when things really light up with a mix of sounds including Latin, mainstream and reggae.
D6 Glyfada 26610 94380

AQUALAND
www.aqualand-corfu.com
This huge water park has 15 adventure pools and slides, tubes, a children's area, shops, cafés, bars and a restaurant. What more do you need? And there are free sunbeds and umbrellas.
D6/E6 Agios Ioannis 26610 58351 May–Oct 10–6 (until 7 Jul–Aug)

ATHENS BAR
The friendly, upbeat owner and staff at this cheerful bar keep things fast paced and make everyone welcome. Big TV screens, pool table, snacks, drinks and great sounds enhance the quirky decor.
A3 Agios Stefanos 26630 51764

BALLOON CLUB
Located inland from the beach, this place flies the flag for clubbing in Agios Georgios with retro-pop and rock and current hits until the early hours.
B4

BOATS RENTAL MARKET
Several options are available if you want to explore the waters round Paleokastritsa. You can hire a self-drive boat or visit the famous sea caves on a cruise. There's even the option of a trip on a glass-bottomed boat.
B5 Paleokastritsa 69774 09246/69761 60370

COCONUT BAR
Cocktails aplenty smooth the night away at this hot spot where DJs spin a mix of old and new favourites.

SUNSET VIEWS

The Cycladic island of Santorini has built a career on sunset views and they are certainly spectacular. But Corfu's west coast offers sunsets that are every bit as eye-catching. The region does not go in too much for full on dance venues and the evening scene here is a more relaxed music, bar and drinks. You can enjoy the sunset from almost anywhere, but the higher the better. Great sunset spots include hilltop Pelekas, the cliffs at Peroulades, Lakones and Angelokastro.

A3 Arillas 26630 51150

CORFU GOLF CLUB, ERMONES
www.corfugolfclub.com
Cricket is already established on Corfu, so why not a round of island golf?
C6 Ropa Valley 26610 94220

DIVING FUN CLUB
www.corfudivingfunclub.gr
In stunning surroundings above and below water, this well-established beachside business offers a one-day beginners' course, PADI training and open water and advanced open water and Divemaster courses.
B4 Agios Georgios 26630 96092 May–Oct

DIZZY'S BAR
Relax with evening drinks at Ermones to mainstream sounds, Latin and 1960s favourites.
C6 Ermones

LA GROTTA
www.lagrottabar.com
A perennial favourite for drinks and relaxing, not least for its great location in a rocky cave with tempting swimming. The music covers just about everything going. It's down 142 steps opposite the Paleokastritsa Hotel.
B5 Paleokastritsa 26630 41006

HAWAII BAR
www.hawaiipelekas.com
After sunset drinks you

can enjoy the 70s to 90s sounds in the lively sports bar.
D6 Pelekas 26610 94451

MALIBU
Open from late until the early hours, the Malibu is a busy cocktail bar that leans towards retro rock and pop. Satellite TV sports add to the draw and there's internet access.
A3 Arillas 26630 51243

ODYSSEY DIVERS
Scuba diving is organized from a beachside base. Enjoy dives from the beach or go by boat.
C6 Ermones Beach
26610 94241

PELEKAS CAFÉ
www.pelekascafe.com
Right at the heart of Pelekas is this popular venue that makes for a great coffee stop by day and a lively cocktail and drinks venue by night. Things go on until the early hours and you're guaranteed to be on your dancing feet by midnight.
D6 Pelekas 26610 95104

ROPA VALLEY RIDING STABLES
Easy riding through the lush environs of the Ropa Valley is available at this centre attached to the golf club (▷ 81).
C6 Ropa Valley, Ermones 26630 94220

SAN STEFANO BOAT HIRE
www.san-stefano.gr
Rent a self-drive boat that gives you the freedom of the sea south to Paleokastritsa and north to Sidari.
A3 Agios Stefanos
26630 51910

SAN STEFANO TRAVEL
www.san-stefano.gr
Take to the ocean on a boat trip to Paleokastritsa (▷ 72–73) or the Diapontia Islands (▷ 76) or even as far as Paxos (▷ 96–97), the Greek mainland or Albania.
A3 Agios Stefanos
26630 51910

SAN STEFANOS WATERFRONT DIVE CENTRE
www.divingincorfu.com
A relatively new venture staffed by fully qualified staff, this diving centre has outstanding venues for all levels of diving and offers training courses.
A3 Agios Stefanos
26630 51108

DIVING

The best way of enjoying diving in the clear waters and among the spectacular sea caves and reefs of Corfu's west coast is to book a trip with a reliable local diving company. If you are very experienced, however, and choose to dive independently you should never dive in working harbours or around yacht mooring areas. It is also wise to seek advice from local divers about any restrictions on diving in environmentally sensitive areas.

SEVENTH HEAVEN CAFÉ
Part of the Panorama Restaurant above Longas Beach, this is where you toast the setting sun.
B2 Longas, Peroulades
26630 95035 All day

SIMPLE BEACH CLUB
Stylish decor at this beachfront place goes with great cocktails and drinks and music that rolls along between chill-out and rock into the small hours.
A3 Agios Stefanos
69364 16979

SUN FUN CLUB
At the south end of the beach the Sun Fun Club offers fun watersports, Jet-skis, paragliding, self-drive boats and skippered cruises.
B4 Agios Georgios
26630 96355

SUNSET BAR
www.levanthotel.com
Enjoy sunset drinks at the bar of the Sunset Mediterranean Restaurant of the Levant Hotel (▷ 84). Look east and you may see the lights of Corfu Town.
D6 Pelekas 26610 94230

Restaurants

PRICES

Prices are approximate, based on a 3-course meal for one person.
€€€ over €25
€€ €15–€25
€ under €15

ALOHA BEACH CLUB (€)

A useful all-day pitstop, this beachside place offers breakfast, lunch, and *mezes* in the evening.
D6 Glyfada Beach 26610 94380 All day

DAS BLAUE HAUS (THE BLUE HOUSE) (€€)

www.das-blaue-haus.com
The views from the balcony of this bright and airy place are worth a visit alone and the delicious food makes things even better. The mixed salad with wild herb dressing is a must for starters, mains are subtly prepared and they do delicious desserts.
A3 Afionas 26630 52046 May–mid-Oct from 3pm

BROUKLIS (€€)

www.brouklis.com
A devoted clientele proves the quality of this classic taverna that wins you over with such treats as *kolokithorita*, delicious 'pumpkin pie', and with its great range of Corfiot cuisine. It even has WiFi.
A3 Arillas 26630 51418 Lunch, dinner

DELFINI (€€–€€€)

Dine out on terrace overlooking the sea. They cater for breakfasts, snacks and full meals. Good fish dishes include lobster when available.
B4 Agios Georgios 26630 96323 All day

ELIA (€–€€)

An attractive restaurant-bar, Elia is on the way down to the beach. They have pasta and pizza on the menu as well as grills and local standards.
D6 Myrtiotissa All day

ELIZABETH'S (€)

For the simplest and tastiest of Corfiot dishes, Elizabeth's at the lovely village of Doukades can still deliver after many years of popularity. Mainly indoor eating although a couple of tiny tables put you right on the village street if you fancy the full Greek experience shared with the passing world.
C4 Main street, Doukades 26630 41728 Lunch, dinner

CORFU COCKEREL

Corfu cuisine has had many influences over the centuries and has produced some enduring favourites. The great Corfiot dish *pastitsada* derives from Venetian *spezzatino* and is made with meat or veal cooked in wine, red wine vinegar and tomatoes with a wonderful array of garlic, spices, cloves, paprika and cinnamon. Layered pasta plays its part and the whole dish is topped off with cheese. True Corfiot *pastitsada*, however, is made with cockerel.

FIGARETO (€€–€€€)

A fixed-price buffet of delicious food is the prize at Louis Grand Hotel's main restaurant on Glyfada Beach. You can relax while you feast on the terrace overlooking the beach.
D6 Glyfada 26610 94140 Dinner

FISHERMAN'S CABIN (€€–€€€)

Eat with adventure at this unique location south of Agios Georgios Beach. It takes about 20 minutes to walk along a track from the south end of the beach. A torch for the return trip is advised or take a taxi boat.
B4 Agios Georgios 26942 585550 Mon–Fri 4pm–11pm, Sat–Sun 1.30pm–11pm

GOLDEN FOX (€€–€€€)

www.corfugoldenfox.com
This popular place offers one of the best views in Corfu. From high above Paleokastritsa savour the view along with local favourites or splash out on *astakos* (lobster).
B4 Lakones 26630 49101 Lunch, dinner

JIMMY'S (€–€€)
www.jimmyspelekas.com
If you want the best of Corfiot favourites such as *sofrito* and *stifado* then this is the place. A long family tradition keeps the standard high.
D6 Pelekas 26610 94284 Apr–Oct lunch, dinner

LIMANI (€–€€)
Down by the harbour Limani offers excellent local dishes. There's a tasty fish *meze* for two and a useful menu for children. The leafy terrace is fringed with roses.
B5 Paleokastritsa Harbour 26630 42080 All day

MARINA RESTAURANT (€€)
www.hotelmarina.gr
Attached to the hotel of the same name, this spacious and comfortable place does local cuisine and has some tasty vegetarian options also. There's a popular Greek night each Saturday.
A3 Arillas 26630 51100 All day

NAFSIKA (€–€€)
The menu here covers all bases with Greek and Mediterranean cuisine and international touches.
A3 Agios Stefanos 26630 51051 Lunch, dinner

NAFSICA RESTAURANT (€€)
Great sunsets, great traditional food including fresh fish dishes makes this a popular place. Try the king prawns in garlic.
C6 Ermones Golf Palace Hotel, Ermones 26610 94045 All day

NEREIDS (€€)
This outstanding venue has a big garden courtyard and stylish decor. The food measures up with such Greek treats as *bekri meze* (meat in a wine and tomato sauce with herbs), and there are delicious desserts. You may even get a lively dancing show from the friendly waiting staff.
B5 Main road, Paleokastritsa 26630 41013 Lunch, dinner

THE NIGHT OWL (€)
A cheerful, unfancy roadside taverna in a wooded setting, The Night Owl is a traditional grillroom that dishes up tasty local favourites and keeps going throughout the year.
A3 Afionas 26630 51314 May–Oct daily lunch, dinner; Nov–Apr daily dinner

DESSERTS

There has never been a great tradition of 'desserts' in Greece. Small dishes and a big main course of meat and fish were the robust staples in Greek villages. Today, international influences have seen a rich palette of desserts in the more expensive restaurants, but in tavernas, fresh fruit is often available or you could settle for an old favourite, the delicious *giaourti kai meli*, yoghurt with honey.

SUNSET MEDITERRANEAN RESTAURANT (€€–€€€)
www.levanthotel.com
High-level eating at this superb location at the Levant Hotel (▷ 111). The food is modern Greek with international choice too.
D6 Pelekas 26610 94230

TAVERNA BIKOLIS (€€)
Charcoal grill is the style at family-run Bikolis, where they bake their own bread and offer pizzas as well as excellent Greek standards. There's a lovely central fire to warm you up on cool evenings.
B2 Sidari road, Peroulades 26630 95291 Dinner

TAVERNA O MANTHOS (€€)
This long-established restaurant overlooking the beach does Corfiot specialties, grills and barbecued food.
A3 Agios Stefanos 26630 52197 Lunch, dinner

Southern Corfu

The narrow southern part of Corfu has long sandy beaches along its western coast and there are several popular resorts. Inland, at villages such as Agios Mattios, the authentic spirit of an older Corfu survives.

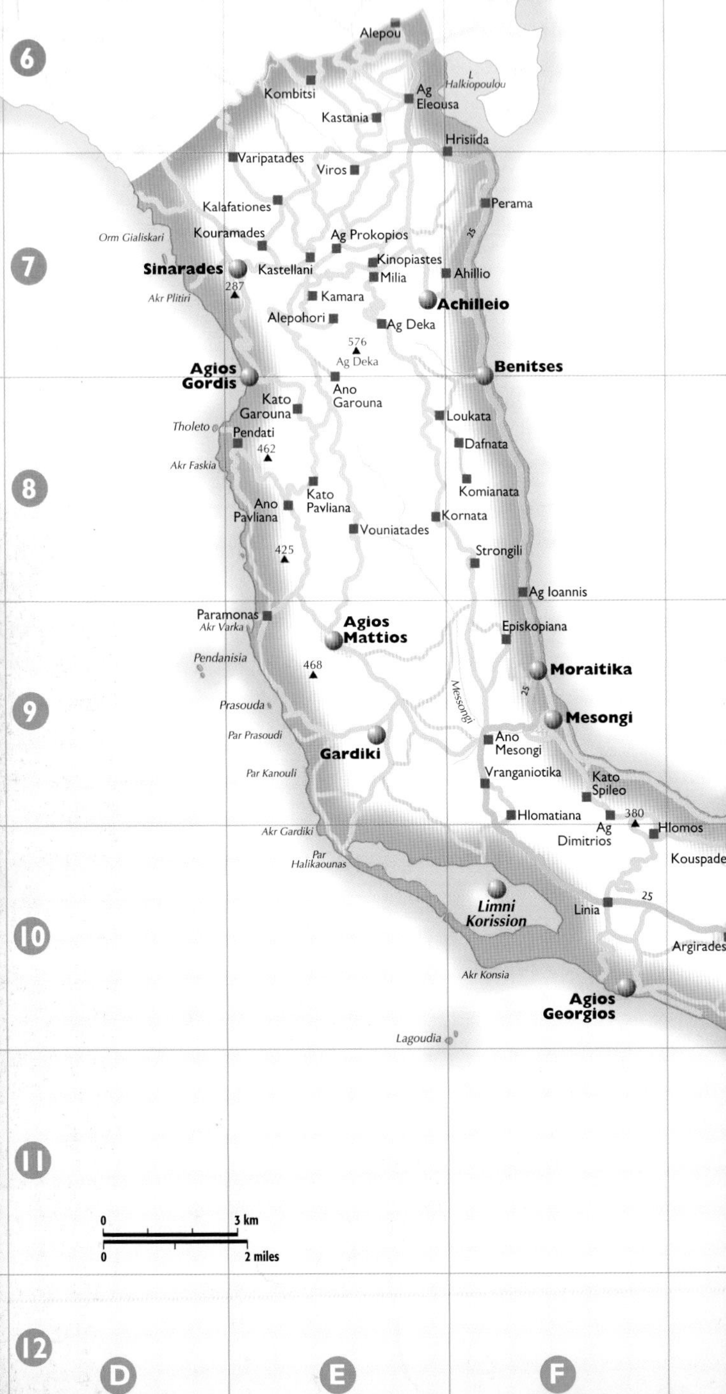
6
7
8
9
10
11
12
D
E
F
Alepou
L Halkiopoulou
Kombitsi
Ag Eleousa
Kastania
Hrisiida
Varipatades
Viros
Perama
Kalafationes
25
Orm Gialiskari
Kouramades
Ag Prokopios
Kinopiastes
Sinarades
Kastellani
Milia
Ahillio
287
Akr Plitiri
Kamara
Achilleio
Alepohori
Ag Deka
576
Ag Deka
Agios Gordis
Ano Garouna
Benitses
Kato Garouna
Loukata
Tholeto
Pendati
Dafnata
462
Akr Faskia
Komianata
Kato Pavliana
Ano Pavliana
Kornata
Vouniatades
425
Strongili
Ag Ioannis
Paramonas
Akr Varka
Agios Mattios
Episkopiana
Pendanisia
468
Moraitika
Messongi
25
Prasouda
Mesongi
Par Prasoudi
Gardiki
Ano Mesongi
Par Kanouli
Vranganiotika
Kato Spileo
Hlomatiana
380
Ag Dimitrios
Hlomos
Akr Gardiki
Par Halikaounas
Kouspade
Limni Korission
Linia
25
Argirades
Akr Konsia
Agios Georgios
Lagoudia
0
3 km
0
2 miles

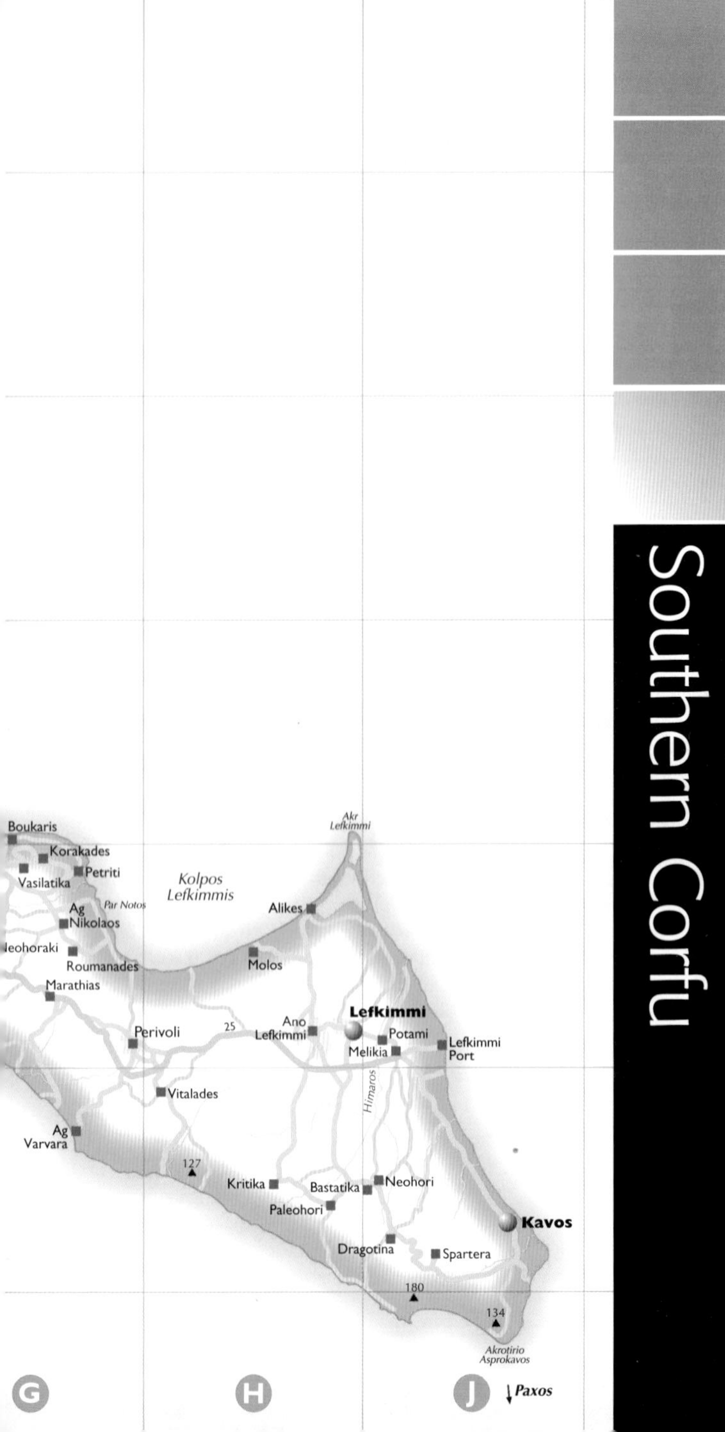
Southern Corfu
Boukaris
Korakades
Vasilatika
Petriti
Kolpos Lefkimmis
Ag Nikolaos
Par Notos
Akr Lefkimmi
Alikes
Neohoraki
Roumanades
Molos
Marathias
Lefkimmi
Ano Lefkimmi
25
Perivoli
Potami
Melikia
Lefkimmi Port
Himaros
Vitalades
Ag Varvara
127
Kritika
Bastatika
Neohori
Paleohori
Kavos
Dragotina
Spartera
180
134
Akrotirio Asprokavos
G
H
J
Paxos

Achilleio

HIGHLIGHTS

- Gardens
- Views
- Statues
- Vivid colours

TIPS

- Visit early or late in the day to avoid tour bus crowds.
- Check for the Kaiser's 'saddle throne'.

The Achilleion Palace is a glorious mix of neoclassicism, ancient references and imperialist fantasy, all of it verging on exquisite bad taste. Enjoy it all, together with a royal promenade round the Palace's beautiful garden.

Imperial beauty The Achilleion represents the indulgence and, some might say, decadence of 19th century European Imperialism. It was built in the early 1890s as a retreat from the fraught world of the Viennese court by the star-crossed and fascinating Elizabeth of Wittelsbach (1837–98) who became Empress of Austria and Queen of Hungary. Known affectionately as Sisi, the Empress was a great beauty who seems to have had a self-regard that matches those of today's narcissistic top celebrities. Elizabeth created the Achilleion as a tribute to her fantasy hero, Achilles.

Clockwise from far left: A sculpture in the grounds; columns and statues on the terrace; a view of the palace from the grounds; inside the palace; one of the palace's reception rooms;

In 1898, aged 60, she was stabbed to death on the lakeside at Geneva by an anarchist randomly seeking a royal victim.

Famous figures The Achilleion was bought in 1907 by Kaiser Wilhelm II, who expanded the Achilles theme, not least by installing a monumental statue, *Achilles Triumphant*, to balance Sisi's sentimental marble, the *Dying Achilles*. There are numerous other statues, including a row of Muses, a sensuous *Leda and the Swan*, and the topsy-turvy musician Arion clasped by the dolphin that saved him from the sea. Among sedate statues of real-life poets, philosophers and orators are Euripides with his nose knocked off and a dashing Shakespeare. On view inside the palace are the ornate entrance hall, the Empress's chapel, and ground-floor reception rooms containing furnishings and memorabilia of Empress and Kaiser.

THE BASICS

E7
Gastouri village
26610 56610
Apr–Oct daily 8–7; Nov–Mar daily 8.30–3
Cafés near entrance
Blue Bus No. 10 from San Rocco Square, Corfu Town–Achillion–Gastouri
Few
Moderate
Limited parking. Many tour buses congregate during morning and early afternoon

Agios Gordis

The sweeping bay (left); a small boat pulled free of the water (right)

THE BASICS

E8

About 12km (7 miles) southwest of Corfu Town

Good choice of cafés and tavernas

Green Bus from Avramiou Street, Corfu Town–Agios Gordis

Few

HIGHLIGHTS

- Views
- Sun, sea and sand
- Watersports
- Nightlife

Corfu's beaches spoil you for choice, especially on the west coast, where the sand is golden, the beaches are big and the living is easy. Agios Gordis is one of the best.

Scenic sands Apart from its golden sand and fine bathing, Agios Gordis definitely takes the prize for a magnificent setting that is second only to Palaiokastritsa's (▷ 72–73) awsome backdrop of mountains. The beach at Agios Gordis is framed by big headlands to north and south. At the northern end of the beach is Plitiri Point and a rocky outcrop known as Aerostato, or Vardia, The Lookout. It was used, as the name implies, as a watch point for the pirates who plagued the Ionian islands during the medieval period and for Ottoman invaders hell bent on adding Corfu as the final prize in their occupation of Greece. They never quite managed to.

Family fun Lying just offshore from the precipitous Cape Faskia at the southern edge of Agios Gordis is the dramatic tusk-like pinnacle known as the Ortholith. There is a similar tree-covered pinnacle onshore and smaller rock outcrops on the beach.

Behind it all, the wooded slopes of Mount Garouna rise majestically to the skies. Agios Gordis beach is a lively place in high season, but if you visit during May and early June there's plenty of breathing space. There are watersports available and there is good snorkelling at the north end of the beach.

The harbour (left); Roman ruins (right)

Benitses

One of Corfu's first resorts, Benitses has a noble pedigree that embraces Ancient Greece, the Roman era, European Royalty and British rule. Add your own legacy to the roll call.

Reputation regained For years Benitses endured fairly raucous, off-the-wall tourism and its name suffered, but the village has won back a more balanced reputation. There were always two Benitses, however, and the brash resort of old was always secondary to the traditional village. Today, fishing caïques still moor with their bows to the harbour walls and on most mornings you can see fish being sold at the dockside. A marina built in 2006 has expanded harbourside life. Across the main road from the harbour, in the village square, there is a big war memorial.

Baths and bridges Kings of the Homeric period are said to have lived in the area and behind the main square lie the ruins of a bathhouse of a Roman villa. A lane leads through the village and onto a network of tracks that climb up wooded slopes where the iron pipes and other remains of a 19th-century British-built water supply still survive. Just north of Benitses Kaiser Wilhelm II built an ornamental jetty for his private yacht and extended it via a bridge over the coast road to steps leading to the Achilleion (▷ 88–89). The bridge was later demolished because highsided vehicles could not pass beneath. The Corfu Shell Museum at the north end of Benitses contains one of the largest shell collections in Europe.

THE BASICS

F7
14km (9 miles) south of Corfu Town
Restaurants and cafés
Blue bus No 6 from San Rocco Square, Corfu Town–Perama–Benitses
Few
Good car parking at harbour. Toilets at village square

Corfu Shell Museum

Main road, Benitses
26610 72227
Apr–Oct daily 9–7.30
Few. The museum is reached by stairs
Moderate

HIGHLIGHTS

- Old buildings
- Woodland walks
- Shell Museum
- Roman baths

Gardiki

TOP 25

HIGHLIGHTS

- Sense of history
- Photography
- Peace and quiet

Brace yourself for time travel at Gardiki. There are traces of the earliest recorded human presence on Corfu, the ruins of a 13th-century Byzantine castle, and a touching reminder of Serbian soldier refugees of World War I.

Ancient walls The ruined Byzantine castle of Gardiki is an atmospheric place, although the empty, overgrown interior is a touch disappointing. The impressive entranceway makes up for it and is reached up rough steps past ancient olive trees. Gardiki may have been built by the mainland Byzantines, who also established Angelokastro fortress (▷ 70–71), as a defence against raids by Genoese pirates, Sicilians and Venetians. A short distance from the castle, on the road from Paramonas and Cape Varka, is a sign indicating the

At Gardiki are the ruins of a Byzantine castle, and the remains of a settlement from 20,000BC

Grava Gardikiou rock shelter, a remarkable relic of the Upper Paleolithic period of 20,000BC. There is a noticeboard alongside the road.

Cave and well The Grava cave signifies the earliest record of human settlement on Corfu from a time when the island was joined to the mainland. Stone tools and animal bones found at the site attest to such use by hunter-gatherers. Orange arrow markers nailed to trees indicate the 400m (346yds) uphill route through olive trees. The cave may seem unremarkable but you are in the presence of 20,000 years of human history. Gardiki's final historical 'signpost' is a short distance along the road from Grava and masked by trees. This is a modest well built for local villagers by grateful Serbian soldiers who were refugees on Corfu during World War I.

THE BASICS

E9

25km (15 miles) south of Corfu Town. Reached from main road at a junction 1km (0.6 mile) west of Moraïtika

Open access

Green Bus from Avramiou Street, Corfu Town–Agios Mattios

None

Free

Limni Korission

HIGHLIGHTS

- Wildlife
- Wide open spaces
- Great beach
- Walking

Where Southern Corfu's tree-covered mountains give way to low-lying coastal plains, Lake Korission gleams in the sun. Birding, beaching, or just being there, is the delightful choice.

Fish and birds Lake Korission was once an area of marshland until the Venetian overlords of Corfu built a channel from the sea and created a lagoon fishery and wildfowl resource. The present lake covers 607ha (1,500 acres) and fish trapping is still carried out at the southern end. Countless migrating birds stop off at the lake, which is now a protected wildlife site. A low breakwater, half-covered in sand, and a wide beach separate the lake from the sea. The beach runs for several kilometres to the south and although popular and busy

Clockwise from left: The sand dune beach; the lake is a popular area for birding and is a protected wildlife site

around the lake area, it offers an escape from the crowds if you are willing to trek south for a couple of kilometres (around 1.6 miles).

Vivid flowers Stands of silvery-green juniper lie scattered along the lake shores and dense thickets of reed waver in the breeze. More than a dozen species of orchid grow here as well as lilac-coloured sea holly, sand lily and various spurges. Korission is a paradise for birders, especially in spring and autumn. More than 120 species have been recorded here. They include widgeon, ibis, cormorant, great white egret, red-backed shrike and little egret. Less welcome winged visitors also flourish in the area. Inevitably, Lake Korission is a breeding ground for biting insects, so make sure you cover up and take repellent.

THE BASICS

F10

On the west coast about 20km (12 miles) south of Corfu Town

Open access

Taverna at north end of lake

Green Bus from Avramiou Street, Corfu Town–Agios Mattios. Get off at Gardiki junction, then a 3.5km (2-mile) walk from here

Paxos

TOP 25

HIGHLIGHTS

- Relaxed pace
- Views
- Walks
- Boat trips

TIPS

- Make sure you visit the Paxox Museum in Gaios.
- The 'Green Man' statue at the south end of the harbour is of local hero Georgios Anemogiannis, a ship's captain who died aged 23 in a battle during the Greek War of Independence.

An Ionian gem, the island of Paxos lies 48km (30 miles) south of Corfu. This is where you change down a gear without even trying to. The island casts its spell. Leaving is the hardest part.

Hidden corners In classical mythology Poseidon is said to have chopped off the southern tip of Corfu and then towed it south to make a hideaway for himself and his lady, Amphitriti. Paxos is 11km (7 miles) long and 5km (3 miles) wide. Its highest point is Megali Vigla, St. Isavros at 250m (820ft). Olive trees, Corsican pines and cypresses cover the island in a green pelt and in spring the air is sweet with the scent of wild flowers. Tiny villages hide at the end of dusty lanes and other tracks and paths lead to remote coves and beaches. The west coast of the island has

The waterfront at Gaios (left); olive trees provide the important crops of oil and fruit (right)

spectacular cliffs, sea caves and wind-sculpted rock formations.

Village gems The Venetians came to Paxos and built a fortress on the island of St. Nicholas. The island sits in the bay of Gaios and protects the town from too much sea. Paxos now has three main settlements all linked by buses. There is bright and cheerful Gaios, the island 'capital' on the southeast coast. The lovely, low-key Longos is further north on the east coast while laid-back Lakka lies at the northern tip of the island. Just south of Paxos is Antipaxos, 3sq km (1.2 square miles) in size and a mini-gem in its own right. It can be reached by ferry boat. Swathed in olive groves and noted for its wine, this tiny island has several idyllic little beaches, although you share the idyll in high season.

THE BASICS

Off map at J12

60km (37 miles) southeast of Corfu Town

Numerous cafes and restaurants

Daily fast ferries to and from Corfu town in summer. Car ferries to and from Corfu Town via mainland Igoumenitsa. Daily sea planes between Gouvia Bay and Paxos

Few

Paxos Magic Holidays www.paxosmagic.com

26620 32269

Another good travel agent is Gäios Travel www.gaiostravel.co.uk

26620 32033

More to See

AGIOS GEORGIOS

Agios Georgios' narrow beach is part of an almost continuous 12km (7.5-mile) ribbon of golden sand fringing the coast south from Lake Korission (▷ 94–95). Things can be a little breezy at times, but crystal-clear waters and the chance of escaping the crowds to either side makes up for it.

F10 35km (22 miles) south of Corfu Town Tavernas and bars Green Bus from Avramiou Street, Corfu Town–Argirades–Agios Georgios (one per day, summer) Few

AGIOS MATTIOS

Agios Mattios, one of Corfu's largest mountain villages, climbs part way up the forested slopes of Mount Agios Mattios, 463m high (1,519 ft). A track leads to the summit and to an abandoned monastery still cared for by villagers. The main street is a lively bustle of people and traffic, but a higher street leads to a peaceful church in a lovely square with spectacular views.

E9 15km (9 miles) south of Corfu Town Cafés, tavernas, main street Green Bus from Avramiou Street, Corfu Town–Agios Mattios Few

KAVOS

Kavos is Corfu's premier over-the-top fun resort for young people although families with young children enjoy the safe bathing. Nights are manic, but fun, although the downside is the binge drinking culture at large. By day there is every kind of water sport, including bungee-jumping to clear your head—or not.

J11 45km (28 miles) south of Corfu Town Snack bars and tavernas Green Bus from Avramiou Street, Corfu Town–Kavos Few

LEFKIMMI

Lefkimmi is a long straggle of linked villages. A narrow road leads north to old salt pans at Alykes and to Akra (Cape) Lefkimmi, noted for its bird life. From the northern part of the village a long main street leads past old Venetian-style houses to Potami,

The church of St. Arsenios in Lefkimmi (left); Limni Korission (above)

Night-time in Kavos

where the road crosses the River Himaros. The south bank of the river is a paved promenade.

H10 · 40km (25 miles) south of Corfu Town · Cafés and tavernas · Green Bus from Avramiou Street, Corfu Town–Kavos · Few

MESONGI

Mesongi is a neighbour of Moraitika but separated by the Mesongi River and well away from the main road. The sand and shingle beach is narrow but has safe bathing. Hotels, villas and tavernas line the beach but everything is low key and friendly.

F9 · 22km (14 miles) south of Corfu Town · Cafés and tavernas · Green Bus from Avramiou Street, Corfu Town–Kavos · Few

MORAITIKA

This popular resort has a long, narrow sand and shingle beach. There are watersports in plenty with gentler variants for children. The busy main road section of the resort is packed with cafés, tavernas and shops, but the charming old village of Ano Moraitika, its pretty houses draped in bougainvillea, lies tucked away at the north end of the resort.

F9 · 20km (12 miles) south of Corfu Town · Cafés and tavernas · Green Bus from Avramiou Street, Corfu Town–Kavos and Corfu Town–Mesongi · Few

SINARADES

There is a strong community spirit in Sinarades and colourful festivals are sustained by the village's own Philharmonic orchestra that performs in the pretty central square, where there are huge palm trees and a statue featuring rearing horses. Opposite the Church of St. Nicholas an alleyway leads to the charming Folklore Museum of Central Corfu.

E7 · 15km (miles) from Corfu Town · Cafés and tavernas · Green Bus from Avramiou Street, Corfu Town–Sinarades–Agios Gordis · Few

Folklore Museum of Central Corfu

2 Nikokavoura Street · 26610 54962 · May–Oct Mon–Sat 9.30–2 · None · Inexpensive

The harbour at Moraitika

Interior of the Folklore Museum of Central Corfu in Sinarades

Coast and Country

Take in the east coast resorts of Southern Corfu and then cross to the hillier west coast and the agricultural village of Agios Mattios.

DISTANCE: 73km (47 miles) **ALLOW:** 4 hours, but more with stops or diversions

START

CORFU TOWN
F6

1 Take the main road south following signs for Lefkimmi. In about 4km (2.5 miles), at a busy T-junction, go left, signposted Lefkimmi. Continue to Benitses and Moraitika.

2 At the south exit to Moraitika, go right and after about 1km (0.5 mile), at a junction, keep round left and go over a bridge. At a junction beside a garage, go right and follow signs to Agios Mattios (▷ 99) and Pelekas.

3 Agios Mattios makes a pleasant lunch stop. On leaving the village, go left at a junction at its north exit, signposted Paramonas Beach.

4 Keep to the main road. At a junction, where there is a mass of signs, keep straight ahead. Continue past Cape Varka and head south through dense olive groves.

5 Reach the area of Gardiki (▷ 92–93) where you can visit the Grava rock shelter and Gardiki Castle. Divert right for the castle by a stone advertising hoarding. This road also leads to Lake Korission (▷ 94–95).

6 On the main route keep straight ahead to the junction with overhead traffic signs passed on the outward leg.

7 Turn right and reach the junction beside the garage. Turn left and, at the right-hand bend, go straight across the junction and onto a narrow road.

8 Follow this road, enjoying superb views, to reach Agii Deka. Descend through several steep bends, from where there are good views of Corfu Town. At a T-junction go right, signposted Kerkyra, and then follow signs back to town.

CORFU TOWN

END

Shopping

CUORE

Means 'Heart', a fond sentiment that sets the tone for a big range of colourful clothing.
✚ Off map at J12 ✉ Main Square, Gaios, Paxos
☎ 26620 32718

DOLPHINS

Head beyond the tourist gifts and you'll find a fascinating stock of hand-painted replica museum pieces at Dolphins. Hand-made jewellery, wind chimes and other artefacts add to the treasure trove and the same owners run a jewellery shop across the road.
✚ F10 ✉ Agios Georgios, north end ☎ 26620 53022

EARTH COLLECTION

www.theearthcollection.com
Wonderful natural fibre clothing for all the family. Perfect for the heat.
✚ E8 ✉ Moraitika
☎ 26610 77154

EFI'S LEATHER

A big emporium of leather goods, Efi's stocks shoes, bags, belts, wallets, jackets and coats and also jewellery.
✚ F9 ✉ Main Street, Moraïtika ☎ 26610 75911

HELEN'S CORNER

Everything from ceramics to cosmetics is available at this colourful shop that also stocks, clothes, tablecloths, watches, and traditional souvenirs.
✚ E8 ✉ Main road, Agios Gordis ☎ 26610 59074

MADE IN CORFU

Companion to the entertaining Made in Corfu shop near Acharavi (▷ 61), this fascinating place is housed in a very old building that has been rescued by the owner. Check the 'orchestra' of pots and pans hanging from the outside walls. Inside is a cornucopia of old furniture, objets d'art and delicious local food products.
✚ F8 ✉ Main Street, Gastouri ☎ 6948 180198

IL PAREO

Indonesia comes to Paxos at this colourful place on the harbourfront at Lakka. There's a great range of stylish clothing, bags, jewellery and much more, all sourced from the Bali region and very reasonably priced.
✚ Off map at J12 ✉ Lakka, Paxos ☎ 26620 30046

OIL OF THE GODS

Olive oil is famed as the elixir of good health throughout the Mediterranean and, increasingly so, further afield. Homer had words for it, of course. He called it 'liquid gold', although the best oil has more of a greenish tinge. There can be a huge difference in the quality of oil and the chances are that you'll be given fairly standard, imported oil in many restaurants. Extra Virgin Oil comes from the first cold pressing of the olives and is the ultimate 'liquid gold'. Buy authentic locally produced oil to take home with you.

PAXOS OLIVE OIL

You won't get more traditional than this old store near the north end of Gaios harbour. Huge drums and barrels of olive oil from Paxiot vineyards as well as bottled wine from Antipaxos sit beneath dusty open beams.
✚ Off map at J12 ✉ Gaios, Paxos ☎ 26620 32218

SHELL MUSEUM

All types of shells and shell artefacts are sold at the long-established museum whose owner has dived all over the world.
✚ F7 ✉ Main road, Benitses
☎ 26610 72227

VASSILAKIS DISTILLERY SHOP

www.vassilakisproducts.gr
A highly visible outlet opposite the Achilleion Palace gates, the Vassilakis shop stocks a vast selection of wine, spirits and liqueurs, all varieties of kumquat liqueurs as well as kumquat products including marmalade and 'spoon sweets', the syrupy preserves containing fruit or rinds.
✚ E8 ✉ Gastoúri
☎ 26610 34516

Entertainment and Activities

ALOBAR
Popular spot on the beach for some night time action, the Alobar does great cocktails and drinks and also does snacks. Mainstream and modern Greek music and live acts at times.
E8 ✉ Agios Gordis Beach ☎ 26610 53997

BAROCCO
This very hip bar, with smooth decor and furnishings has a huge list of cocktails and flies the flag for Corfu cool.
F9 ✉ Mesongi Beach ☎ 69326 60460

CAFE HARLEY
www.cafe-harley.de
A crazy, lovely garden spills down from the terrace at this drinks venue where they also do food. Try your hand at koja golf, 'adventurous' mini golf in an adjoining garden. Internet access is available and there *is* an old Harley chopper in situ.
F10 ✉ Agios Georgios north end ☎ 26620 52540 Daily 10am–late

CALYPSO DIVING CENTER
www.calypso-diving.gr
Long established, Calypso runs a big range of courses as well as sampler dives for beginners.
E8 ✉ Agios Gordis Beach ☎ 26610 53101/53369

DEEP BLUE
A good late-night hangout and hang-in-there bar-café where the music ranges from easy listening to R&B into the early hours.
Off map at J12 ✉ Harbourfront, north end, Gaios, Paxos ☎ 26620 32767

ERIMITIS SUNSET BAR
The hermit who apparently sojourned at this spot would probably approve of its modern re-creation as one of the coolest nightspots on Paxos. The sunsets are as good as those of Santorini. Great for drinks and they do snacks as well.
Off map at J12 ✉ Magazi, Paxos ☎ 26620 31957

FUTURE
One of Kavos' biggest and most popular venues, Future spins a good mix of sounds from 70s disco to house, while the drinks flow.
J11 ✉ Main street, Kavos

PAXOS MUSEUM

In a world where big city museums and galleries are becoming increasingly artful and chic, places such as the Paxos Musuem are a delight. It's small and the curating is basic, but it gives a great insight into Paxiot history. Farming and domestic artefacts vie with fossils, ancient pottery, guns, coins and clothing. There's a book about Paxos that was written by the Archduke of Austria in 1887. Also within the building are the impressive paintings of the Paxiot priest Christodoulos Aronis.

NAUTILUS DIVING
Nautilus has dive sites on both east and west coasts and also has a base at Agios Georgios.
F9 ✉ Mesongi Beach Hotel ☎ 26610 83045 or 689777 53499

PAXOS MUSEUM
Housed in a one-time school building this wonderful museum (see box) should not be missed.
Off map at J12 ✉ Gaios Harbourfront, Paxos ☎ 26620 32556 May–Oct daily 10–2, 6–10; one hour later in summer Inexpensive Stepped access

ROCKY'S
Among the legion of Kavos bars, Rocky's proves a great favourite with its open air venue, all the latest hits and unrelenting partying.
J11 ✉ Main Street, Kavos ☎ 694424600

XL INTERNET AND SPORTS CAFÉ
This busy and lively venue is big and brash and has a pleasant balcony overlooking the beach. Plenty of drinks and snacks, plus pool, music and big-screen TV keep the place going.
F10 ✉ Agios Georgios south end ☎ 26620 51779 Daily 10am–late

Restaurants

PRICES

Prices are approximate, based on a 3-course meal for one person.

€€€ over €25
€€ €15–€25
€ under €15

ALONAKI BAY TAVERNA (€€)

A legendary taverna in a great location above the sea with tables scattered amid clustering trees. Good Corfiot home cooking, with fish a specialty.
E10 Just north of Lake Korission 26610 75872/76118 Lunch, dinner

ARAGHIO (€€)

Friendly service and a good local chef at this charming place add to the joys of tasty fish dishes, such as fish soup, seafood pastas and fish *mezes* plates. Meat dishes are also available.
Off map at J12 Gaios, Paxos 26610 32521 Lunch, dinner

LA BOCCA (€€)

An end of the road delight is this dreamy venue overlooking a small beach and backed by dense greenery. Very Italian-orientated with international touches.
Off map at J12 Lakka, Paxos No phone Lunch, dinner

CAPRICCIO (€)

A smart little harbour road place, Capriccio dishes up crepes, ice creams and drinks of all kinds. It's the perfect people-watching venue.
Off map at J12 Gaios, Paxos 20972 856111 (mobile)

THE DRUNKEN SQUID (€–€€)

Go for the hot stuff, the tacos, burritos and enchiladas, at this well-run Tex-Mex outfit where friendly, efficient service and generous helpings are the order of the day.
J11 Main Street, Kavos 26620 61192 Lunch, dinner

FISHERMAN'S HAUNT (€–€€€)

Fish are the thing here, although meat dishes and pasta are also available. Try fish soup or calamari followed by fresh fish of the day.
F9 2km (1 mile) south of Mesongi 26610 75365 Lunch, dinner

FEAST OF FISH

Fish may be expensive, but it is irresistible and Corfu is the place for it. For starters, try *marides*, whitebait fried whole in olive oil then sprinkled with sea salt and lemon. A universal Greek favourite is *calamari*, fried squid. *Bianco* is an Italian-inspired *bouillabaisse*, casserole of whiting or grey mullet cooked with potatoes, garlic, lemon juice and herbs.

KAFESAS (€€)

With a mini fleet of local boats catching their fish, Kafesis, not surprisingly, has a deserved reputation for seafood. It also has dozens of delicious *mezes* on offer.
F10 Agios Georgios, south end 26610 51196 Lunch, dinner

PIZZA GARDEN (€–€€)

A no-nonsense pizza place that does not stint on the helpings, you can eat on the premises here, or take it away.
J11 Main Street, Kavos 26620 61064 Dinner

O PAXINOS (€€)

Friendly, family-run O Paxinos covers all the traditional dishes in a bright, immaculate interior. Casserole dishes are superb and there's a great range of *mezes* and local fish when available.
F7 Benitses Old Village 26610 72339

THE RIVER (TO POTAMI) (€)

Blessed by the Blessed Rick Stein in his *Mediterranean Escapes* television programme, the owners of this classic taverna have let nothing go to their heads. The kitchen still turns out unfancy but delicious local food and the menu stays simple.
J10 Lefkimmi-Potamos, south side of bridge 26620 22958 All day

CAFE

THE ROSE GARDEN (€–€€)
The charming Rose Garden lives up to its name with its rose-covered terrace. There's a mighty plate of cold and hot Greek Cypriot-style *mezes* to satisfy anyone, or try *stamnas*, beef cooked in a pot with red wine and feta.
F9 Main Street, Moraitika 26610 75622 Lunch, dinner

SEA BREEZE (€€)
This popular beachside taverna offers Greek favourites and dishes with general Mediterranean and international touches.
E8 Agios Gordis Beach 26610 53214 Lunch, dinner

SEBASTIAN (€–€€)
A terrific menu covers starters such as big olives stuffed with meat or fish and rolled in breadcrumbs. The wood-oven-baked pizzas are heart-shaped and the pasta is fresh. Try one of Nancy's famous home-made desserts and you'll never leave.
F10 Agios Georgios, north end 26620 52008 Lunch, dinner

SPIROS KARIDIS (€€–€€€)
They know their fish and how to prepare it at this popular *psarotaverna*. A generous helping of shrimps makes for a good starter, then choose your main treat and savour it within sight of the little harbour full of fishing boats.
G9 Boukaris harbour 26620 51205 Lunch, dinner

STAMATIS (€–€€)
One of the best country tavernas, where the food is outstanding and the *mezes* are a meal in themselves. Cheerful service, impromptu music and the very persuasive house wine, made by the owners, add to the pleasure.
E7 Viros (near Vrioni) 26610 39249 Dinner. Closed Sun

TAVERNA DIONYSOS (€–€€)
Big helpings and an unbeatable beachside location make this bright, cheerful place a great bet for everything from breakfasts to sandwiches, snacks, pizzas, lunch and dinner.
F9 Mesongi Beach 26610 49081 All day

MEAT TREAT

Grilled meat is a perennial favourite in Greece, and Corfu is no exception. At simple tavernas, the grill is rarely cold. *Souvlaki* is skewered grilled meat, often interspersed with peppers and, at its best, flavoured with herbs. The best *souvlaki* is with *arnisia*, lamb, while *hirini*, pork, is also tasty.

TRIPA TAVERNA (€€–€€€)
One of Corfu's most famous eateries, Tripa's boasts a past guest list that includes François Mitterand and Jane Fonda plus a host of celebrities from A to Z. *Mezes* are generous in quality and quantity and the mains likewise. Spit-roasted lamb or the legendary *kleftiko*, lamb baked in parchment to seal in the juices, are favourites. The desserts and wine list live up to expectations, while Greek dancing entertains.
E7 Kinopiastes 26610 56333 Dinner

VASILIS (€€)
The menu at harbourfront Vasilis is part of a replica newspaper of the 1970s, a lovely touch that reflects the delicious traditional fare of local and Greek regional dishes as well as pasta and risotto.
E7 Loggos 26620 30062 Lunch, dinner

ZEPHYROS (€€)
There are flowers and greenery everywhere at this relaxing and well-run beachfront taverna. Dishes are Corfiot favourites with subtle international touches.
E8 Agios Gordis Beach 26610 59079 Lunch, dinner

Where to Stay

Corfu's accommodation options range from basic resort 'boxes' to luxurious mega-hotels in private grounds. Between is a range of Corfu Town hotels and an increasing number of self-catering apartments and villas scattered throughout the island.

Introduction

Most visitors to Corfu stay in the resorts scattered around the island and many hotels and apartments are block-booked by travel companies. There is still a huge choice for independent travellers, however. Corfu Town does not have many hotels and in the centre these tend to be mid-range to luxury. Some resort rooms are no more than 'box and balcony' places with cramped space and tiny balconies. Other places are excellent and maintain a loyal clientele.

Getting the Best Price

Prices for most hotels, but especially the less upmarket places, can vary greatly, depending on the time of year. As always, Easter and August are the busiest and most expensive periods, when you'll pay the full rate. Early in the year is especially good for discounts, when owners are pragmatic. When booking ahead ask for confirmation in print. Hotels and rooms must display their legally agreed prices.

What to Expect

Hotel 'grading' in Greece is becoming rather blurred as accommodation options increase and modernization blurs the differences in levels of facilities. Many modern apartments within budget and mid-range price bands can be exceptionally well appointed. Very big resort hotels can have boring rooms and balconies with little separation between. There should be en suite facilities with towels in most places and each room should have a balcony. Remember that hotels advertising 'sea views' are usually talking about the front rooms.

BOOKING ONLINE

It is worth checking internet sites before booking rooms. Local sites, including those in this guide (▷ 115) have good information on hotels and apartments outside Corfu Town. General sites include www.laterooms.com, www.expedia.com and www.lastminute.com. For self-catering try www.holiday-rentals.co.uk. Many hotels and apartments listed in this guide have their own websites.

From the top: Nisaki beach; hotel reception; a hotel on Erikoussa; Bella Mare Hotel, Avlaki

Budget Hotels

PRICES

Expect to pay under €70 per night for a double room in a budget hotel.

ATHENS BAR ACCOMMODATION

These spacious, well-equipped apartments just behind the beach have clever design touches.
F2 Agios Stefanos
26630 51764

BRETAGNE

The Bretagne is a modern hotel with 43 comfortable, well-appointed rooms. It is within walking distance of the airport and has its own bar and restaurant. Corfu Town centre is about 1.5 km (1 mile) away.
F6 Georgaki 27, Garitsa 26610 30724

CAMPING PALEOKASTRITSA

www.paleokastritsaholidays.com
Standing on a series of old olive tree terraces, this well-run and well-equipped campsite is on the approach road to Paleokastritsa beach. It has 103 pitches. They can also arrange rooms and apartments nearby.
B5 Paleokastritsa
26630 41204 Mid-May to mid-Oct

DALIA

www.daliahotel.com
A decent, functional hotel of 17 rooms just a few minutes from the airport and overlooking the local sports stadium. Scenic is not the word, of course.
Off map at a5
National Stadium Square, Garitsa, Corfu Town
26610 32341

HOTEL MARINA

www.hotelmarina.gr
The 16 rooms at this beachfront hotel are bright and fresh and have double-glazed windows and unbeatable sea views from their balconies. There is a lift to the upper floors, a ground-floor restaurant and a swimming pool.
A3 Arillas 26630 51100-1 May–Oct

PENSION MARTINI

www.pensionmartini.com
Pension Martini has been welcoming repeat guests to Pelekas for many years, not least for the friendly and helpful owners and the quirky character of the property. Do not expect swish mod cons, but plenty of character instead.
D6 Pelekas
22610 94326
Apr–Oct

PASSPORT

You will be asked for your passport by hotel reception and by room owners when you check in. This is an understandable guarantee of payment, but you should wait for the necessary details to be recorded and for your passport to be returned to you, rather than collect it later. Recommended hotel and room owners are to be entirely trusted, but it is better to keep your passport on side all the time.

THE RIVER ROOMS

Behind the taverna of the same name in Potamos are six self-catering apartments surrounded by a classic Greek garden. If you're happy with basic, unvarnished accommodation, the prices, even in August, are truly budget.
J10 Lefkimmi-Potamos
26620 22958

VILLA MON AMOUR–KOKKINOS

A charming place in a lovely garden setting at the southern edge of Arillas and about 300m (330yds) from the beach, Villa Mon Amour's seven studios and apartments all come with kitchens, and there's a children's playground.
A3 Arillas 26630 51106 Apr–Oct

VILLA MYRTO

www.villamyrto.com
There is outstanding value and quality at these lovely self-catering rooms in a very quiet location near Myrtiotissa Beach (▷ 77). The pool and bar are a great bonus.
D6 Pelekas 26610 95082 Mar–Oct

Mid-Range Hotels

PRICES

Expect to pay between €70 and €150 per night for a double room in a mid-range hotel.

ACHARAVI BEACH HOTEL

www.acharavibeach.com

The 78 apartments and bungalows of this custom-built hotel overlook the beach and there are swimming pools and a tennis court.

D2 Acharavi Beach 26630 63102 Apr–Oct

APOLLO PALACE HOTEL

This large attractive hotel has a selection of 290 rooms, studios and suites within a large garden complex. There are two main pools and a children's pool and playground and an open-air amphitheatre. Various activities are organized daily and the beach can be reached through the garden.

F9 Mesongi 26610 75433 Apr–Oct

APOLLON HOTEL

www.corfu-apollon-hotel.com

A well-kept resort hotel of 42 rooms just across the road from the beach at Paleokastritsa. Friendly service, pleasant rooms and a general upbeat style make this a good choice.

B5 Paleokastritsa 26630 41211 Mid-May–Oct

ARCADION

www.arcadionhotel.com

A handsome Venetian façade in spite of the well-known fast-food outlet on the ground floor distinguishes this Corfu Town hotel right on the Spianada. There are 73 comfortable rooms, the front ones having great views of the evening *volta* (promenade) around the Liston of an evening.

b2 21 Vlasopoulou Street, Corfu Town 26610 37670

ATLANTIS

www.atlantis-hotel-corfu.com

A bleak-looking frontage masks good modern accommodation at this 61-room hotel near Corfu Town's busy New Port.

Off map at a1 48 Xenofondos Stratigou, Corfu Town 26610 35560

BREAKFAST

Breakfast may or may not be included within the overall price of a hotel. The more upmarket hotels tend to include breakfast, which can vary from a fairly basic choice of rolls, bread, cake and jam to the full buffet choice of juices, fruit, yoghurt, cereals, ham, cheese and boiled eggs. Coffee and tea are always available. The British custom of fried breakfast accompanied by large amounts of tea is not entirely recognized in Greece.

BELLA VENEZIA

www.bellaveneziahotel.com

This comfortable Corfu Town hotel occupies a neo-classical mansion that was formerly a girls' high school. Its 31 rooms were refurbished in 2006. Breakfast is in a lovely garden pergola.

b3 Zambeli 4, Corfu Town 26610 46500

BOUNIAS APARTMENTS

Tucked away near the lovely Avlaki Beach, these quiet rooms and apartments are good value and are only 2km (1.2 miles) from bustling Kassiopi.

F2 Avlaki 26630 81183/ 26610 24333 Apr–Oct

CASA LUCIA

www.casa-lucia-corfu.com

A unique complex of cottages located about 12 km (7.5 miles north-west of Corfu Town on the Paleokastritsa road (▷ Box).

B5 Sgombou 26610 91419 Apr–Oct

CHRISTINA HOTEL

www.christina-hotel.com

This excellent 16-roomed hotel has an enviable beachside location. Rooms are comfy and very clean and there's a bar and restaurant.

F9 Mesongi Beach 26610 76771 May–Oct

GOLDEN FOX

www.corfugoldenfox.com
There are unbeatable views from the 11 rooms at the Golden Fox complex high above Paleokastritsa. The adjoining restaurant is a bonus.
B4 Lakones 26630 49101

KASSIOPI BAY HOTEL

www.kassiopibay.com
An outstanding location on the tip of Cape Kassiopi to the north of Kassiopi town makes this attractive hotel a good centre from which to explore the scenic north east of Corfu. There is a selection of 24 self-catering rooms and studios.
F2 Kassiopi 26630 81713 Mid-Apr to mid-Oct

KONSTANTINOUPOLIS

www.konstantinoupolis.gr
This handsome old building overlooking Old Port Square reflects classic old Corfu Town architecture. The 31 comfortable rooms have been modernized but with style and the spiral wooden stairs are a nice touch.
b1 11 Zavitsianou, Corfu Town 26610 48716

LEVANT HOTEL

www.levanthotel.com
Occupying an unbeatable position high above Pelekas and the western sea, this hotel has ultimate peace and quiet. The 25 rooms are traditionally decorated and facilities include internet access.
D6 Pelekas 26610 94230 Apr–Oct

MOLFETTA

www.molfettabeach.com
Located at the heart of busy Gouvia, this attractive hotel has 27 bright and comfortable rooms set within a charming garden with the shingle beach just yards away.
D5 Gouvia 26610 91915 May–mid-Oct

PAXOS BEACH HOTEL

www.paxosbeachhotel.gr
Located about 1.5km (1 mile) south of Gaios, the main settlement of Paxos, these 42 attractive bungalows are in a marvellous location on terraces stepping down to the seashore.
Off map at J12 Gaios, Paxos 26620 32211 Apr–Oct

CASA LUCIA

Set amidst an old olive grove these 10 self-catering studios and cottages were converted from an original olive press complex and now stand amidst beautiful and extensive gardens around a central swimming pool. Each unit has its own unique style, colour scheme and decor and all have great character. Casa Lucia enhances its ethos of calm and creativity by offering Yoga, pilates and T'ai Chi sessions while musical and other cultural events are often held. Longer lets are available in winter at very reasonable prices.

SAINT NICHOLAS

www.saint-nicholas-hotel.com
There's a touch of class about this hotel on the Mazis family estate where service is attentive. There are two swimming pools, a children's play area and a stylish restaurant and bar.
E5 Gouvia 26610 91621/2

SAN GIORGIO ROOMS

Located at the entrance to Paxos' main settlement as you come from the port, these seven apartments and rooms are perched on a hillside and have good views. The rooms are fresh and uncluttered and have basic cooking facilities.
Off map at J12 Gaios, Paxos 26620 32223 May–Oct

ZEPHYROS

www.hotel-zefiros.gr
A longstanding, popular Paleokastritsa hotel since the 1930s, the 11-roomed Zephyros has been beautifully renovated in recent years. Rooms have stylish decor and there is a friendly welcome.
B5 Paleokastritsa 26630 41244 Apr–Oct

Luxury Hotels

PRICES

Expect to pay between €150 and €250 per night for a standard double room at a luxury hotel.

BELLA MARE

www.belmare.gr

Located at the north end of Avlaki Beach (▷ 57), this lovely hotel has the tranquillity often lacking in busy resort hotels. The 21 self-catering apartments are bright and spacious and the grounds have a lovely swimming pool.

F2 ✉ Avlaki Beach ☎ 26630 81997 Apr–Oct

CAVALIERI

www.cavalieri-hotel.com

The Cavalieri is located in a 17th-century mansion overlooking Corfu Town's famous Spianada. It has 50 rooms, and although some are a touch small, all have class and character and the front rooms have a fine outlook. The roof terrace has panoramic views.

b3 ✉ 4 Kapodistriou, Corfu Town ☎ 26610 39041 Apr–Oct

CORFU PALACE

www.corfupalace.com

This modern luxury hotel has 115 rooms and suites and overlooks Garitsa Bay just down from Corfu Town's famous Spianada. There is a beauty and fitness centre, two swimming pools, two restaurants and large well kept grounds.

b3 ✉ 2 Leoforos Dimokratias, Corfu Town ☎ 26610 39485

KONTOKALI BAY HOTEL

www.kontokalibay.com

In beautiful grounds and dominating the wooded Kontokali Peninsula (▷ 58) north of Corfu Town, this big hotel of 243 rooms is ideal for families, not least because of its pool two private beaches, watersports and children's club.

E5 ✉ Kontokali ☎ 26610 99000 Late Apr–Oct

LOUIS CORCYRA BEACH HOTEL

www.louishotels.com

Part of the Louis Hotel chain, this luxurious place has 370 units and commands a veritable estate of grounds and private beaches. Facilities include swimming pools and Jacuzzi and a fun pool for youngsters. There's a range of water sports on the nearby beach.

D5 ✉ Gouvia ☎ 26610 90196 Apr–Oct

OLD CORFU

The Villa de Loulia is a classic example of a more gracious Corfiot age. The main building dates from 1803, when it was built by 'Grandmother Loulia', an ancestor of the present owner. Its style is Italianate, its garden surroundings are beautiful and serene. Each of the nine rooms and suites bear names such as Persephone or Pandora and each has a unique decor. Sun-drenched, peaceful corners and a swimming pool add to the pleasures.

LOUIS GRAND HOTEL

www.louishotels.com

With 232 rooms and 15 suites this big hotel dominates Glyfada beach. Rooms are big and the entire hotel has a relaxed spacious style. Lush gardens lead to the beach.

D6 ✉ Glyfada ☎ 26610 94140–5 Apr–Oct

SIORRA VITTORIA

www.siorravittoria.com

Corfu Town's most stylish boutique hotel is housed in an early 19th century mansion. Each of the 9 rooms and 2 suites has individual decor and names. There is a garden courtyard. Breakfasts are delicious.

b2 ✉ 36 Stefanou Padova, Corfu Town ☎ 26610 36300

VILLA DE LOULIA

www.villadeloulia.gr

There's more than a touch of gracious Corfiot living at this delightful small hotel (▷ box). Dinner is available if booked ahead.

B2 ✉ Peroulades ☎ 26630 95394/mob 69329 71558 May–Oct

Need to Know

The practicalities of a holiday in Corfu are straightforward, although there are some aspects of Greek life that a visitor might find strange at first. There is nothing daunting about this. It's a case of being prepared to go with the flow.

Planning Ahead

When to Go

Ideal times to visit are late April to late June and early September to mid-October when it is not too hot and there are fewer visitors. Late June, July and August are the busiest times and temperatures are very high. Easter is a moveable feast but is vibrant with celebration and festival.

TIME

Corfu is two hours ahead of Britain, 7 hours ahead of New York and 10 hours ahead of Los Angeles.

AVERAGE DAILY MAXIMUM TEMPERATURES

JAN	FEB	MAR	APR	MAY	JUN	JUL	AUG	SEP	OCT	NOV	DEC
57°F	59°F	61°F	66°F	74°F	82°F	88°F	90°F	82°F	74°F	66°F	61°F
14°C	15°C	16°C	19°C	23°C	28°C	31°C	32°C	28°C	23°C	19°C	16°C

Spring (March–May) Generally mild but with occasional bouts of very cold and wet weather from the northeast.
Summer (June to mid-September) becomes increasingly hotter with days of unbroken sunshine. There can be unexpected spells of rain and thunderstorms, however.
Autumn (Mid-September to November) There is often an extended summer, with sea temperatures at their highest, but there is an increasing chance of rain at any time.
Winter (December–February) prolonged dull wet weather is common, but with periods of mild sunny days. Cold spells from the north and east.

WHAT'S ON

February/March Pre-Lenten carnival season in the three weeks prior to Ash Wednesday. Numerous village festivals. Major carnival in Corfu Town on Sunday before Ash Wednesday. The Monday before Ash Wednesday is *Kathari Deftera*, 'Clean Monday', with picnics and kite flying.
8 March *St Theodora's Day*, procession in Corfu Town.

April *Easter* (moveable).
Palm Sunday: the remains of St Spyridon are carried around Corfu Town.
Good Friday: numerous religious processions.
Easter Saturday: The ancient tradition of pot-throwing from Corfu Town balconies. Fireworks display.
Easter Sunday: parades, processions, celebrations throughout island.

May May 1 *National Holiday*.
May 21 *Union with Greece*. Procession in Corfu Town.

June *Pentecost Sunday/ Whit Monday*: village festivals.
June 29: *Festival of St. Gaios* on Paxos.

July *Corfu Music Festival*.
July 26 *Feast of St Paraskevi*, celebrated at Avliotes, Agios Mattios, Benitses, Ipsos and Kinopiastes.

August August 6 *Saviour's Day*. Pilgrimages in preceding week to Mount Pandokrator, festival in Campiello.
August 11 *St Spyridon's Day* procession in Corfu Town.
August 15 *Assumption of the Virgin*. Village festivals.

September Late September/ October, *Corfu Festival*.

October *Ohi Day*.
Celebrates refusal by Prime Minister Metaxas of Mussolini's 1940 request to march Italian troops through Greece.

Corfu Online

www.allcorfu.com
This comprehensive site covers history, culture, activities, accommodation, travel to and within the island and more. It has links to other sites.

www.corfunet.com
A useful site for accommodation and for general information about the island. It has a link to a site about Agios Stefanos, northwest.

www.terrakerkyra.gr
A one-time annual travel guide to Corfu has gone online and carries a good mix of information about the island, plus travel.

www.arillas.com
A good local site for Arillas resort.

www.paxos-greece.com; www.paxos.tk
Information about Paxos and the practicalities of getting to the island.

www.agni.gr
Takes you to 'The Corfu Travel Guide' and to masses of information about the island.

www.corfutrail.org
Everything you need to know about the Corfu Trail and about the island's options for walkers.

www.paleokastritsa.biz
A developing site about Paleokastritsa and area, with good accommodation information.

www.culture.gr
'Odysseus' is the official portal of the Hellenic Ministry of Culture, carrying information about museums and archaeological sites.

www.ferries.gr
A very useful site for information on all Greek ferries including ferry connections with Corfu.

GOOD TRAVEL SITES

www.greeka.com/ionian
A general Greece guide that has good travel information, accommodation and other links for Corfu and around.

www.fodors.com
A complete travel-planning site. You can research prices and weather; reserve air tickets, cars and rooms; ask questions (and get answers) from fellow travellers.

CYBERCAFÉS

Bits & Bytes
Busy and buzzing with youngsters on internet games, but connections are good.
✉ Corner of Mantzarou and Rizospaston Voulefton, Corfu Town
☎ 26610 36812
🕒 8am–1am
€1 for 20 minutes

Netikos
Slightly worn surroundings, including keyboards, but good connections.
✉ 12–14 Kaloxairetou, Corfu Town (behind north end of Liston)
☎ 26610 47479
🕒 Daily 10am–late
€1 for 20 minutes

Getting There

ENTRY REQUIREMENTS

For the latest passport and visa information check the UK Foreign Office website at www.fco.gov.uk or the US Department of State at www.state.gov

TOURIST OFFICES

Corfu does not have a particularly useful official information resource, though this may yet change. There are tourist information kiosks in San Rocco Square and at the south end of the Liston. In recent years they have been open during the late spring and summer.

● For general information: Greek National Tourism Organisation, Athens ☎ 21033 10392; www.gnto.gr
GNTO offices, Corfu Town ✉ Rizopaston Vouleuton ☎ 26610 37520 ✉ Evangelistrias 4 ☎ 26610 37520

● Most travel agencies offer advice, but understandably are interested mainly in business from customers. In Corfu Town, a reliable agency for all your needs is All Ways Travel ✉ 35 Plateia G Theotoki Square (San Rocco Square) ☎ 26610 33955; www.corfuallwaystravel.com

AIRPORTS

Corfu Airport is 3km (2 miles) south of Corfu Town centre. For information ☎ 26610 89600. The arrival hall is not large and can become very crowded during summer. Facilities include a currency exchange kiosk, a bank, an ATM, car rental desks, a shop and basic refreshments.

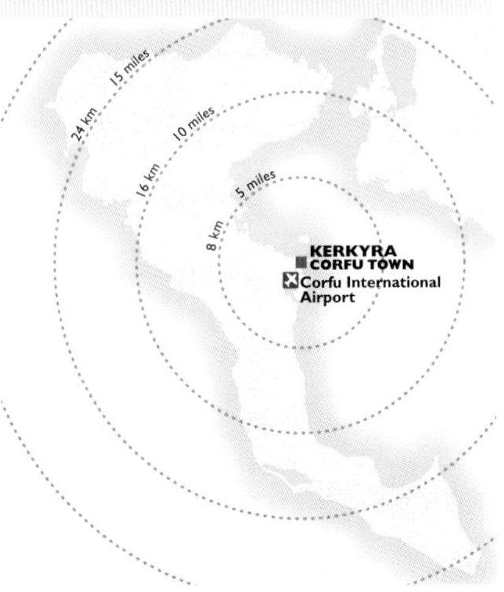

ARRIVING BY AIR

Corfu Airport has a very busy schedule from mid-May to October, especially on Mondays and Fridays. Charter flights make up most of the traffic, but there are scheduled daily flights from Athens. Currently (2009) there are direct EasyJet flights from London during the main holiday season. Main local operators are Olympic Airways (Athens to Corfu flights) ☎ 26610 38187; www.olympicairlines.com; Aegean Airlines ☎ 26610 27100; www.aegeanair.com. EasyJet operate flights from London to Corfu (www.easyjet.com).

● The Arrivals Hall has an information desk. Airline company desks operate only for pre-flight check-ins. You will usually have long waits for luggage during busy periods. There is no left-luggage facility.

● Local buses stop outside the airport to take you into Corfu Town. Taxis wait outside the

airport (€10 to town centre). There may be a surcharge for luggage. Check what the charge is before getting into a taxi. It is possible to walk into the centre of town but it takes about 30 minutes. Go right, on reaching the main road at the airport entrance. Pass the sports stadium and in about 800m (875yds) reach the seafront and turn left.

ARRIVING BY BUS

There are daily KTEL buses (✉ Avramiou Street ☎ 26610 39985) between Athens and Corfu. The journey takes about 11 hours and the final leg is by ferry (price extra). The journey is an experience in itself, especially if an overnight break is made on the way.

- Corfu buses leave from Athens' Kifisou Avenue Bus Station and terminate at Avramiou Street Bus Station, Corfu Town.
- The company website www.ktel.org has information but only in Greek. The English-language version is under construction.

ARRIVING BY SEA

All ferries operate from Corfu Town's New Port on Ethnikis Antistaseos. Corfu has ferry connections with several Italian ports including Venice (28 hours) and Bari (12 hours). The closest and most frequent service is from Brindisi (8 hours). This service also links Corfu with the Greek mainland port of Patra.

- Agoudimas Lines (Corfu) ✉ 1 Ethnikis Antistaseos ☎ 26610 80030; www.agoudimos-lines.com
- A daily high-speed SNAV ferry (www.snav.it) links Corfu, Paxos and Brindisi from July to early September.
- An hourly car ferry runs between Igoumonitsa on the mainland and Corfu Town and less frequently between Igoumonitsa and Lefkimmi.

ARRIVING BY CAR

If bringing your own vehicle a ferry crossing to Corfu is necessary. See Arriving by Sea, above.

INSURANCE

Check your insurance policy and buy any necessary supplements. EU nationals receive reduced cost emergency medical treatment with the relevant documentation (EHIC card for Britons) but full travel insurance is advised and is essential for all other visitors.

CUSTOMS

Provided it is for personal use, EU nationals can bring back as much as they like although you should be aware of add on costs for baggage operated by some airlines. Current guidelines are: 800 cigarettes, 200 cigars, 1kg tobacco, 10 litres spirits, 20 litres of aperitifs, 90 litres of wine.

ADVICE

- It is impolite to make negative comments in public about the Greek religion, culture or the Greek State. The police have been known to treat such matters as potential offences.
- Nude bathing is illegal in Greece although some beaches are officially designated as 'naturist'. 'Topless' bathing by woman is the norm on many beaches, but respect sensibilities when off the beach and near religious institutions.

Getting Around

DRIVING TIPS

Local drivers may push to overtake, regardless of being on a main road or a narrow lane. Do not increase speed. It is often best to slow down and pull in when you can. But do not pull off abruptly onto a likely lay-by. There is often a sharp drop where the edge of the road ends.
When meeting another vehicle at a constricted section of road, if the opposing driver flashes their headlights it is not an invitation for you to proceed. It means that they are about to do so.
If you find a village street is becoming ever more narrow, retrace your route before it becomes a donkey track.

VISITORS WITH A DISABILITY

Corfu's Old Town, the Campiello, is not easy for those with mobility problems. There are numerous stairs and steps throughout. The Spianada (Esplanade) and the Liston, and the streets behind the Liston, however, are very accessible for wheelchairs. There are not many buildings with facilities for those with mobility problems. Resorts are generally on level ground and many beaches have wooden rampways in summer.

Corfu has a good local bus service, as in all of Greece. The network is extremely useful for those visitors who do not want to rent a car. Alternatively, most resorts organize coach excursions and some resorts operate small bus services to and from beaches. There are car and scooter rental outlets throughout the island.

BUSES

URBAN TRANSPORT (BLUE BUSES)

Blue Buses (☎ 26610 31595) operate from San Rocco Square and serve Gastouri, (Achillion), Kondokali, Gouvia, Dassia, Benitses, Pelekas, Kanoni and villages within central Corfu. Tickets are purchased at a kiosk beside the bus station.

ISLAND TRANSPORT (GREEN BUSES)

Corfu's rural bus service is run by the national bus company, KTEL and services operate from Corfu Town to numerous destinations. Buses do not always go to the centre of resorts and may simply stop on the main road, anything up to a kilometre or two away. Buses can be boarded anywhere along country roads and tickets are purchased on board.
The KTEL Terminus is at Avramiou Street, Corfu Town ☎ 26610 39985.

DRIVING IN CORFU

Corfu's main road network is good although it does not always have the precise road markings of other countries. Rural roads can be very narrow and can be down to single-width in places and through some villages. Rural roads can have some axle-crunching potholes, so drive slowly and be alert. If using a hire car it is not advised to drive on unsurfaced roads and tracks. Mountain roads often have spectacular multiple hair-pins.

- Driving is on the right-hand side of the road.
- Use of seat belts is compulsory.
- Always carry your driving licence.
- Children under age 10 should not ride in a front seat.

Drink driving is a very serious offence in Greece and random checks by police are increasing. A blood alcohol level of 0.05 brings an instant fine. Over 0.09 is a criminal offence for which you may be jailed. Don't drink and drive. The speed limit is 100kph (62mph) on main highways, 90kph (56mph) on lesser main roads and 50kph (31mph) in built-up areas.

There are car rental outlets at Corfu Airport and numerous outlets in Corfu Town and in all resorts. Most hotels can put you in touch with reputable rental firms. Always check the car thoroughly in front of rental personnel. A reliable and helpful local company is: International Rent-a-Car ✉ 20a Kapodistriou ☎ 26610 33411/37710

AIRSEALINES

AirSealines (www.airsealines.com) operates daily seaplane flights to Paxos (About €36 single). The trip takes about 20 minutes. There is free transport to and from the AirSealines office in Corfu Town to Gouvia Marina.

GUIDED TOURS

There are numerous coach trips to various places throughout the island. You can book through resort outlets or through your hotel.

TAXIS

In Corfu Town there are taxi ranks at the Airport, the Spianada (Esplanade), San Rocco Square and the New Port. For radio taxis, ☎ 26610 33811. Fares are higher for trips from Corfu Town to resorts and between midnight and 6am. Luggage is surcharged. Blatantly inflated charges should be questioned. If not satisfied, phone the Tourist Police.

STUDENTS AND SENIOR CITIZENS

An International Student Identity Card (ISIC) can provide reductions in entrance prices to museums and historic sites. Senior citizens enjoy reduced rates for the same.

PAXOS

From May until about mid-September daily high-speed, passenger-only hydrofoils run between Corfu Town and Paxos. The trip takes one hour (Petrakis Lines ✉ Ethnikis Antistaseos ☎ 26610 31649).

PHOTOGRAPHY

Bringing back the memories is all part of the holiday experience, but there are certain courtesies that should be adopted. Flash photography in churches and museums is often disapproved of. Please respect this and, if unsure, ask an official or attendant. If you want to photograph any local person, especially in villages, think about whether or not you are intruding on their privacy and ask their permission. Avoid taking photographs near military installations or of military personnel on exercise. The authorities are very sensitive about this and arrests have taken place.

Essential Facts

POSTAL SERVICES

There are post offices in Corfu Town and at the larger resorts. Post boxes are yellow.

Main Post Office, Corfu Town

✉ Junction Alexandras and Zafiropoulo 🕑 Mon–Fri 8–2

MONEY

The Euro (€) is the official currency of Greece. Notes are in denominations of 5, 10, 20, 50, 100, 200 and 500 euros and coins are in denominations of 1, 2, 5, 10, 20, 50 cents and 1 and 2 euros.

5 euros

10 euros

50 euros

100 euros

ELECTRICITY

The power supply throughout Greece is 220 volts Ac, 50Hz. Sockets are equipped for twin round-pin plugs. Visitors from Britain should bring an adapter and US visitors require a voltage transformer.

MEDICAL AND DENTAL TREATMENT

- Medications that contain codeine are restricted in Greece. If you carry such medications it's best to take a prescription record, although it is highly unlikely that you will be questioned over prescribed medications.
- If you use prescribed medicines it is advisable to carry a prescription record.
- Dental treatment needs to be paid for. Make sure you have insurance cover.
- Ask your hotel or letting agent for details of local doctors. Most resorts have a medical resource. Some resorts have very busy clinics.
- Corfu Town Hospital ✉ 1 Andreadi Street ☎ 26610 88100 (emergencies 26610 88223 for surgical, 26610 88267 for pathology)
- Corfu Town General Clinic ☎ 26610 36044

MONEY MATTERS

- Most Greek national banks have branches in Corfu Town and all have ATMs. Bigger resorts have subsidiary branches of the main banks and a growing number of resorts have ATMs.
- Cash and travellers' cheques can be exchanged in banks and in some travel agencies. Banks generally give better rates.
- Credit cards are widely accepted in shops and in some restaurants, but cash in hand is still very much a part of Greek life so it is wise to have cash with you especially in resorts.
- Car rental usually requires credit card use.

OPENING TIMES

- Shops open 9–2, 5–9 in summer. Museums and archaeological sites are open 10–2. Some places stay open throughout the day.
- Other usual opening times are: offices 9–5; banks 8/9–2; pharmacies 9–2, 5–6.30

POLICE

- Corfu is generally unthreatening and safe, but there can be exceptions.
- If you feel you have a genuine grievance against a service or facility, report the matter to the Tourist Police.
- If you are victim of, or witness to a crime, contact the regular police.

PUBLIC HOLIDAYS

1 Jan New Year's Day
6 Jan Epiphany
Feb/Mar Kathari Deftera/Clean Monday/Shrove Monday (41 days before Easter)
25 Mar Independence Day
Mar/Apr Holy Week celebrations
1 May Labour Day
Late May/early June Holy Spirit Day
15 Aug Feast of the Assumption
28 Oct Ohi Day
25/26 Dec Christmas Day/St Stephen's Day

TELEPHONES

- To make a call from a street telephone you need a phone card, *telekarte*. These can be bought for a few euros at small local shops, souvenir shops and at *periptera* (street kiosks).
- You can also phone at the OTE, the national phone company office in Corfu Town (3 Mantzarou). Most mobile phones adjust to Greek service providers but international calls are expensive.
- It is worth buying a rechargeable SIM card while you are in Greece.
- Using a mobile phone while driving is prohibited.
- International Dialling Codes:

Dial 00 followed by
UK 44
USA/Canada 1
Ireland 353
Germany 49
Italy 39
France 33

EMERGENCY NUMBERS

Police 112 or 100
Fire 112 or 199
Forest Fire 112 or 191
Ambulance 112 or 166

Tourist Police
✉ 4 Samartzi Street (off San Rocco Square)
☎ 26610 30265/39503

Hospital
✉ 1 Andreadi Street
☎ 26610 88110 (for emergencies dial 26610 88223)

CONSULATES

Australia
☎ 210 870 4000 (Athens)
Canada
☎ 210 727 3400 (Athens)
France
☎ 26610 42905 (Corfu)
Germany
✉ 23 Kapodistrou, Corfu Town ☎ 26610 31453
Ireland
✉ 20a Kapodistriou, Corfu Town ☎ 26610 33411
Italy
✉ 7 A Vraila , Corfu Town
☎ 26610 37351
UK
✉ 18 Mantzarou Street, Corfu Town ☎ 26610 23457
USA
☎ 210 721 2951 (Athens)

Language

The official language of Corfu is Greek but most Corfiots involved with tourism speak English fluently. However, it can be useful – and courteous – to know a few words of Greek, especially in rural areas. Knowledge of the Greek alphabet is useful for reading street names and road signs.

ACCOMMODATION	
hotel	*xenodhohío*
room	*dhomátyo*
....single	*....monó*
....double	*....dhipló*
for three people	*ya tria átoma*
Can I see it?	*Boró na to sho?*
breakfast	*proinó*
guest house	*pansyón*
toilet paper	*charti iyías*
toilet	*twoléta*
bath	*bányo*
shower	*doos*
hot water	*zestó neró*
balcony	*balkóni*
campsite	*kamping*
key	*klidhí*
towel	*petséta*

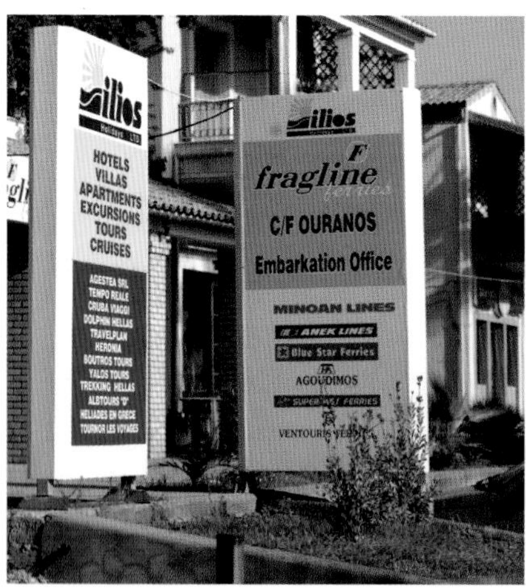

MONEY MATTERS

bank	*trápeza*
exchange office	*ghrafío sinalóghamatos*
post office	*tahidhromió*
money	*leftá*
cash desk	*tamío*
how much?	*póso kóni*
exchange rate	*isotimía*
credit card	*pistotkí kárta*
travellers' cheque	*taxidhyotikí epitayí*
passport	*dhiavatíryn*
Can I pay by…?	*boró na pliróso me…*
cheap	*ftinós*
expensive	*akrivós*

EATING OUT

restaurant	*estiatório*
café	*kafenío*
menu	*menóo*
lunch	*yévma*
dinner	*dhípno*
dessert	*epidhórpyo*
waiter	*garsóni*
waitress	*servitóra*
the bill	*logHariazmós*
bread	*psomi*
water	*nero*
wine	*krasi*
coffee	*kafés*
tea (black)	*tsáli*

PUBLIC TRANSPORT

aeroplane	*aeropláno*
airport	*aerodhrómio*
bus	*leoforío*
…station	*…stathmós*
…stop	*…stási*
boat	*karávi*
…port/harbour	*…limáni*
ticket	*isitírio*
…single	*…apló*
…return	*…metepistrofís*
timetable	*dhromolóyo*

USEFUL WORDS

yes	*né*
no	*óhi*
please	*parakaló*
thank you	*efharistó*
hello	*yásas/ yásoo*
good morning	*kalí méra*
good evening	*kalí spéra*
good night	*kalí nikhta*
I don't understand	*thén katalavéno*
goodbye	*adiío/yásas*
sorry	*signómi*
how much?	*póso káni?*
where is…?	*poú eené…?*
help!	*voíthia!*
my name is…	*meh léne…*
I don't speak Greek	*then miló helliniká*
excuse me	*me sinchoríte*
fruit	*fróoto*

CAR TRAVEL

Taxi	*taxí*
car	*aftokínito*
petrol	*venzíni*
the road to	*o dhrómos ya*

Timeline

A GREAT CORFIOT

Count John Capodistrias (1776-1831) was a member of a distinguished Corfiot family. He was Secretary of State for the Ionian Republic and then entered the service of the Russian court becoming Russia's Minister for Foreign Affairs. Capodistrias was a key player at the Congress of Vienna in 1814–15. In 1827 he was elected President of the new Greek state and worked tirelessly to restore and reform the country after centuries of Ottoman control and years of violence. In 1831, he was assassinated at Nafplio in the Peloponnese by opponents of his reforms. John Capodistrias is buried in the Monastery of Platytera in Corfu Town. At Koukouritsa, near the village of Evropouli, 5km (3 miles) west of Corfu Town there is a charming small museum, located in the family home, which celebrates his life.

6000 BC The island is settled by Neolithic hunter-gatherers.

229 BC Corcyra becomes the first Roman colony in Greece.

AD 395 Corcyra comes under the control of the Byzantine Empire.

550 Goth invaders devastate the island.

1081 Corfu is taken over by the Norman King of Sicily.

1148 Corfu is recaptured by the Byzantine Emperor Manuel Comnenus.

1207 Corfu is given to the Venetians.

1214 Byzantines gain control of Corfu.

1267 The Neapolitan House of Anjou gains control of Corfu.

1386 Corfu offers allegiance to Venetians, who rule the island for four centuries.

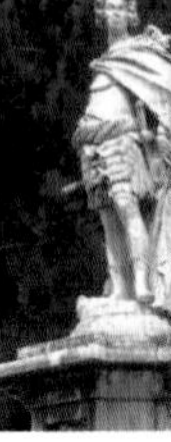

1456 The body of St. Spyridon is brought to Corfu.

1537 First major siege by the Turks.

1715 Second major Turkish siege is repulsed.

1797 The French capture Corfu and the other Ionian Islands.

1814 Corfu becomes part of United States of the Ionian Islands under British Protection.

1864 Corfu becomes part of united Greece.

1940–44 Corfu Town suffers much damage from bombing.

1960s Development of mass tourism.

1981 Greece joins the European Union.

2008 Corfu hosts the International Conference on Information Communication Technologies In Education.

BRITISH PROTECTORATE

Corfu was occupied and influenced by many other countries throughout its history and the British were the last to do so for a protracted period. The Ionian Islands had been occupied by France from 1807 until 1814 and under the Treaty of Paris of 1815 a nominally independent United States of the Ionian Islands was formed, but under British protection. The British did not let go easily. For 50 years Britain was represented by a succession of ten Lords High Commissioners. It was not until 1864 that Corfu became part of an independent Greece.

From left to right: an icon in the Byzantine Museum, Corfu Town; Roman ruins at Benitses; the silver sarcophagus holding the remains of St. Spyridion; statue of Marshal Schulenberg who halted the western spread of the Ottoman empire; Neo Frourio; the Liston; interior view of Mon Repos

Index

TWINPACK
Corfu

WRITTEN BY Des Hannnigan
VERIFIED BY Lindsay Bennett and Penny Phenix
COVER DESIGN Jacqueline Bailey
DESIGN WORK Bookwork Creative Associates Ltd
INDEXER Marie Lorimer
IMAGE RETOUCHING AND REPRO Sarah Montgomery, Michael Moody and James Tims
PROJECT EDITOR Bookwork Creative Associates Ltd
SERIES EDITOR Cathy Harrison

Colour separation by AA Digital Department
Printed and bound by Leo Paper Products, China

A CIP catalogue record for this book is available from the British Library.

ISBN 978-0-7495-6147-5

Published by AA Publishing, a trading name of AA Media Limited, whose registered office is Fanum House, Basing View, Basingstoke, Hampshire RG21 4EA. Registered number 06112600.

Front and back cover images: AA/C Sawyer

A03639
Maps in this title produced from mapping © Freytag-Berndt u. Artaria KG, 1231 Vienna-Austria

The Automobile Association would like to thank the following photographers, companies and picture libraries for their assistance in the preparation of this book.

Abbreviations for the pictures credits are as follows – (t) top; (b) bottom; (c) centre; (l) left; (r) right; (AA) AA World Travel Library.

1 AA/C Sawyer; **2–18** AA/C Sawyer; **4** AA/C Sawyer; **5** AA/C Sawyer; **6tl** AA/S Day; **6tc** AA/S Day; **6tr** AA/C Sawyer; **6bl** AA/M Trelawny; **6bc** AA/C Sawyer; **6br** Photodisc; **7tl** AA/J Tims; **7tc** AA/C Sawyer; **7tr** AA/C Sawyer; **7bl** AA/J Tims; **7bc** AA/C Sawyer; **7br** AA/C Sawyer; **10t** AA/M Trelawny; **10c(i)** AA/C Sawyer; **10c(ii)** AA/C Sawyer; **10b** AA/C Sawyer; **11t(i)** AA/T Harris; **11t(ii)** AA/C Sawyer; **11c** AA/C Sawyer; **11b** AA/C Sawyer; **12t** AA/C Sawyer; **12c(i)** AA/J Davison; **12c(ii)** AA/C Sawyer; **12b** AA/C Sawyer; **13t** AA/C Sawyer; **13c(i)** AA/C Sawyer; **13c(ii)** AA/M Trelawny; **13b** AA/C Sawyer; **14t** AA/C Sawyer; **14c(i)** AA/C Sawyer; **14c(ii)** AA/C Sawyer; **14b** AA/C Sawyer; **15** AA/C Sawyer; **16t** AA/K Paterson; **16c(i)** AA/C Sawyer; **16c(ii)** Stockbyte Royalty Free; **16b** AA/C Sawyer; **17t** AA/C Sawyer; **17c(i)** AA/L K Stow; **17c(ii)** AA/S Day; **17b** AA/A Sattin; **18t** AA/C Sawyer; **18c(i)** AA/C Sawyer; **18c(ii)** AA/C Sawyer; **18b** AA/C Sawyer; **19t** AA/C Sawyer; **19c(i)** AA/C Sawyer; **19c(ii)** AA/C Sawyer; **19b** AA/S Outram; **20/21** AA/C Sawyer; **24l** AA/M Trelawny; **24c** AA/C Sawyer; **24r** AA/M Trelawny; **25l** AA/S Outram; **25r** AA/C Sawyer; **26l** AA/C Sawyer; **26tr** AA/C Sawyer; **26br** AA/C Sawyer; **27t** AA/C Sawyer; **27bl** AA/C Sawyer; **27br**; **28l** AA/C Sawyer; **28c** AA/C Sawyer; **28r** AA/C Sawyer; **29l** AA/J Tims; **29r** AA/C Sawyer; **30t** AA/C Sawyer; **30b** AA/C Sawyer; **30/31** AA/C Sawyer; **32l** AA/C Sawyer; **32r** AA/C Sawyer; **33** AA/S Outram; **34–37 top panel** AA/C Sawyer; **34l** AA/C Sawyer; **34r** AA/C Sawyer; **35l** AA/C Sawyer; **35r** AA/J Tims; **36l** AA/C Sawyer; **36r** AA/C Sawyer; **37l** AA/S Day; **37r** AA/S Outram; **38** AA/C Sawyer; **39–41 top panel** AA/M Trelawny; **42** AA/C Sawyer; **43–44 top panel** AA/C Sawyer; **45** AA/C Sawyer; **48l** AA/C Sawyer; **48r** AA/S Outram; **49l** AA/C Sawyer; **49r** AA/J Tims; **50l** AA/C Sawyer; **50tr** AA/C Sawyer; **50br** AA/C Sawyer; **51tl** AA/C Sawyer; **51tr** AA/C Sawyer; **51b** AA/C Sawyer; **52l** AA/C Sawyer; **52r** AA/J Tims; **53** AA/C Sawyer; **54l** AA/S Outram; **54r** AA/S Outram; **55l** AA/C Sawyer; **55c** AA/C Sawyer; **55r** AA/C Sawyer; **56–59 top panel** AA/C Sawyer; **56l** AA/C Sawyer; **56r** AA/C Sawyer; **57l** AA/J Tims; **57r** AA/C Sawyer; **58l** AA/C Sawyer; **58r** AA/C Sawyer; **59l** AA/J Tims; **59r** AA/C Sawyer; **60** AA/C Sawyer; **61** AA/M Trelawny; **62** AA/C Sawyer; **63–64** AA/C Sawyer; **65** AA/J Tims; **68l** AA/J Tims; **68r** AA/J Tims; **69l** AA/J Tims; **69r** AA/C Sawyer; **70** AA/J Tims; **71t** AA/C Sawyer; **71bl** AA/C Sawyer; **71br** AA/C Sawyer; **72/73t** AA/S Outram; **72bl** AA/S Outram; **72/73b** AA/C Sawyer; **73r** AA/S Outram; **74l** AA/J Tims; **74r** AA/S Outram; **75l** AA/S Outram; **75r** AA/S Outram; **76–77 top panel** AA/C Sawyer; **76l** AA/C Sawyer; **76r** AA/C Sawyer; **77l** AA/C Sawyer; **77r** AA/C Sawyer; **78** AA/C Sawyer; **79** AA/J Tims; **80** AA/M Trelawny; **81–82** AA/C Sawyer; **83–84** AA/C Sawyer; **85** AA/C Sawyer; **88tl** AA/C Sawyer; **88bl** AA/C Sawyer; **88tr** AA/C Sawyer; **88br** AA/S Outram; **89** AA/C Sawyer; **90l** AA/S Day; **90r** AA/S Day; **91l** AA/S Outram; **91r** AA/C Sawyer; **92l** AA/S Outram; **92r** AA/S Day; **94/95t** AA/C Sawyer; **94bl** AA/R Strange; **94/95br** AA/C Sawyer; **95** AA/A Sattin; **96** AA/A Sattin; **97** AA/A Sattin; **98** AA/S Outram; **99–100 top panel** AA/S Outram; **99l** AA/S Outram; **99r** AA/C Sawyer; **100l** AA/S Outram; **100r** AA/S Outram; **101** AA/S Day; **102** AA/M Trelawny; **103** AA/C Sawyer; **104,106** AA/C Sawyer; **105** AA/S Day; **107** AA/C Sawyer; **108–112 top panel** AA/C Sawyer; **108t** AA/M Trelawny; **108c(i)** AA/C Sawyer; **108c(ii)** AA/C Sawyer; **108b** Bella Mare Hotel, Kassiopi–Corfu; **113** AA/C Sawyer; **114–125 top panel** AA/C Sawyer; **120** MRI Bankers' Guide to Foreign Currency, Houston, USA; **122l** AA/C Sawyer; **122tr** AA/S Outram; **122cr** AA/C Sawyer; **122br** AA/C Sawyer; **124l** AA/C Sawyer; **124c(i)** AA/C Sawyer; **124c(ii)** AA/M Trelawny; **124r** AA/M Trelawny; **125l** AA/S Day; **125c** AA/C Sawyer; **125r** AA/C Sawyer.